LOCKHEED'S
BLACKWORLD
SKUNK WORKS

THE U-2, SR-71 AND F-117

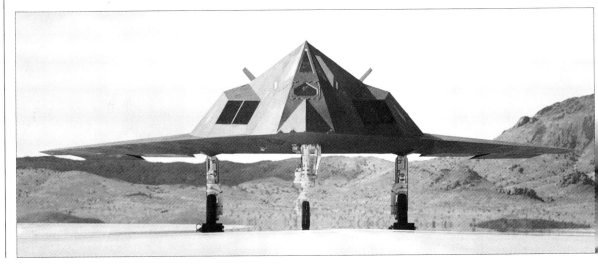

AVIATION PIONEERS

LOCKHEED'S BLACKWORLD SKUNK WORKS

THE U-2, SR-71 AND F-117

PAUL CRICKMORE

First published in Great Britain in 2000 by Osprey Publishing
Elms Court, Chapel Way, Botley, Oxford OX2 9LP, UK
Email: info@ospreypublishing.com

ISBN 1 84176 059 5

Editor: Shaun Barrington
Design: Mark Holt
Origination: Grasmere Digital Imaging, Leeds, UK
Printed in China through Worldprint Ltd

00 01 02 03 04   10 9 8 7 6 5 4 3 2 1

Acknowledgements

The world authority on all written matters U-2, is without doubt,
Chris Pocock. Without access to some of his material, a book of
this nature would have been impossible. For those readers that
wish to delve deeper into the three aircraft types covered in this
book, the author would recommend the following:

Toward the Unknown, by Chris Pocock published by Schiffer.
Lockheed's Skunk Works, by Jay Miller, published by Aerofax.
Lockheed SR-71: The Secret Missions Exposed, by Paul Crickmore,
published by Osprey.
F-117 Nighthawk, by Paul and Alison Crickmore, published by
Motorbooks International.

In addition to thanking Chris for his help, I would also like to
thank Jay Miller, Denny Lombard, Dr Coy Cross, Bobby Wall, Tony
Pennicook and above all my wife Ali for continued enthusiasm
and support.

This book is dedicated to my dear friends Alberto and Karen
Pollicarpo.

Existing and forthcoming books in the Aviation Pioneers series:

X-Planes – Research Aircraft 1891-1970
ISBN 1 85532 876 3

**The Risk Takers - Racing and Record Setting
Aircraft 1908-1968**
ISBN 1 85532 904 2

German and Austrian Aviation of World War I
ISBN 1 84176 069 2

For a catalogue of all books published by Osprey Military
and Aviation please write to:

**The Marketing Manager, Osprey Direct, PO Box
140, Wellingborough, Northants, NN8 4ZA, United
Kingdom
E-mail: info@ospreydirect.co.uk**

**The Marketing Manager, Osprey Direct USA,
PO Box 130, Sterling Heights, MI 48311-0310, USA
Email: info@OspreyDirectUSA.com**

Visit Osprey at **www.ospreypublishing.com**

Contents

Title page Top The clean lines of the U-2R's aesthetically pleasing and dramatic high-aspect-ratio wing is shown here to good effect. (Lockheed Martin)

Title page Middle Five degrees of conical camber is applied to the outboard wing leading edge of the SR-71, to reduce bending movement. The twin fins are canted fifteen degrees inboard to reduce rolling moment due to slide slip and vertical deflection. (Lockheed Martin)

Title page Bottom F117-A aircraft 807 first flew on 13 September 1984 and was delivered to the Air Force on 20 December. (Lockheed Martin)

The U-2

The name of an 11th Century Holy Roman Emperor, Frederick Barbarossa, King of Germany, is etched forever in contemporary history. At dawn on 22 June 1941, Nazi Germany launched Operation Barbarossa, the invasion of the Soviet Union. As its Panzer Divisions rolled east, smashing everything in their path, Soviet industry sought protection deep within the Motherland. Hitler's maps would have been good enough to show him supply lines of a thousand miles to Moscow … When, after WWII, 'An iron curtain … descended across the Continent' and relations between the victorious east and western powers chilled into the Cold War, it was soon discovered that the accuracy of maps and target intelligence held by Britain and the US

was woefully inadequate. With limited human intelligence (HUMINT) being provided by agents in the field, large gaps remained in the knowledge of Soviet industrial and military capability. Stand-off aerial reconnaissance of peripheral targets provided a partial solution to the problem, but the vastness of the Soviet Union left only one option, given the level of technology available at that time - overflight. So began the so called PAROP program - Peace-time Aerial Reconnaissance Operations.

For several years such sorties were conducted utilising converted bombers manned by extremely courageous air crews. De Havilland Mosquito PR.34s flying with 540 Sqn, based at RAF Benson in Oxfordshire, conducted reconnaissance flights from altitudes in excess of 43,000 ft

over such places as Murmansk and Archangel. Operations from such heights provided a haven from interception by Soviet fighters and continued until at least 1949.

In June 1948, the Soviet Union enforced a food blockade upon the western zones of Berlin. The allies responded by mounting a round-the-clock airlift; the United States highlighted the seriousness of the situation by redeploying bombers back to Britain. As allied reconnaissance operations continued, it was only a question of time before such actions provoked the ultimate response. It first occurred on 11th April 1950, when a US Navy Consolidated PB4Y Privateer, operated by VP-26 and with a crew of ten onboard, was shot down and crashed into the Baltic, off Soviet Latvia.

World destabilisation escalateded when at dawn on 25 June 1950, communist North Korea invaded its southern neighbour and in so doing, sparked off the Korean War. In Europe, surveillance operations against the USSR

continued; the 5th Strategic Reconnaissance Group (SRG), from Travis AFB, operated Boeing RB-29s from RAF Sculthorpe and Burtonwood. Like the RAF Mosquitos, their high-altitude performance and long range made them ideal photographic and Electronic intelligence (PHOTINT and ELINT), gathering platforms. In February 1951, a small detachment of four RB-45 Tornados from the 91st SRG, from Lockbourne AFB, Ohio were 'loaned' to Great Britain, painted in RAF markings and were utilised by a mixed USAF/RAF crew on high-altitude, night time overflights of the Soviet Union and Warsaw Pact countries for nearly three years. No aircraft were lost during these nocturnal forays, however, by 1954, developing Soviet anti-aircraft capabilities made it prudent to stop using RB-45s in this role and they were transferred back to USAF control.

Not surprisingly, the Soviet Union were becoming increasingly sensitive to Western incursions into its

Left In the early 1950s North American RB-45C Tornados were loaned by the US government to the RAF, and operated out of RAF Sculthorpe, on clandestine reconnaissance operations. (Paul Crickmore collection)

Top The Canberra PR.7 was an effective high altitude reconnaissance gathering platform during the mid 1950s. (British Aerospace)

Above Despite its highly modified appearance, the Canberra origins of this Martin RB-57F are still readily apparent. (USAF)

airspace and retaliated by pressing home a series of attacks on any aircraft suspected of violating its sovereignty. In April 1952, an Air France DC-4 was attacked and damaged in the Berlin corridor and less than two months later a Swedish Air Force C-47 was downed into the Baltic Sea east of Gotland. Even search and rescue PBY was attacked whilst looking for survivors; the Russians certainly meant business. Four months later, MiG-15s destroyed a reconnoitring RB-29. On 10 March 1953, a USAF F-84 Thunderjet was shot down over Bavaria by Czech MiG-15s. Two days later an RAF Lincoln (RF-531) of the central gunnery school, was shot down in the Berlin Corridor by MiG-15s; seven crew lost their lives. On 15 March 1953, an RB-50 of the 38th SRS, 55th SRW, flown by Lt Col Robert Rich was intercepted by Soviet MiG-15s. The gunner, T/Sgt Jesse Prim, returned fire and the MiG withdrew. However, on 29 July, another RB-50 from the same wing was not so lucky. Attacked by MiG-15s during a reconnaissance flight near the Soviet border, the RB-50 lost a wing and fell into the Sea of Japan. Co-pilot Capt John E Roche was the only survivor.

As the cost in air crew's lives continued to mount it became apparent that a new approach to gathering such vital intelligence was needed. With high altitude having already been established as the 'operational environment' for such missions, it was a US Air Force Major who articulated the way forward. Having spent some time as an aeronautical engineer with Chance Vought, John Seaberg had been recalled to active duty following the outbreak of the Korean War. It was whilst serving as Assistant Chief in the New Developments Office, Bombardment Branch, at Wright Field, near Dayton, Ohio, that he mapped out high altitude strategic reconnaissance philosophy, proposing to mate an aircraft with an extremely efficient high-aspect-ratio wing to the new generation of turbo jet engines. Utilising such a union, he believed an aircraft would be capable of cruising at altitudes far in excess of any other then in service.

Spurred on by his new boss, William Lamar, Seaburg had, by March 1953, created a formal specification, requiring the aircraft to cruise at an altitude of 70,000 feet, possess a range of 1,500 nautical miles, whilst carrying a camera payload weight of up to 700lbs, to be in

Above Undoubtedly two of the world's greatest aeronautical engineers, Kelly Johnson (right) and his protégé, Ben Rich. (Lockheed Martin)

Below Heavily shrouded for security reasons, the prototype U-2 is disgorged from a C-124 at Area 51. (Lockheed Martin)

Bottom Resplendent with 'star and bar' markings, prototype 001 is photographed at Area 51 during very early flight tests. (Lockheed Martin)

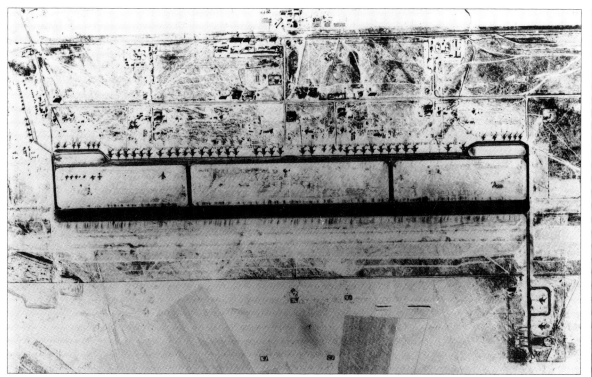

Above The Type A camera system consisted of three Fairchild HR-724, 24-inch cameras carried in the aircraft's 'Q-bay'. (Lockheed Martin)

Top This CIA, U-2 overflight of Engles Air Base, in the Soviet Union, captured 32 Myaseshchev M/4 Bisons and 30 other aircraft dispersed around the airfield. (CIA)

service by 1956. These initial proposals were subsequently released to just three of the smaller aircraft manufacturing companies; the rationale being that as large-scale production was not envisioned, the project would receive a higher priority than if placed with the larger players.

Bell and Fairchild were requested to submit proposals for the design and construction of a totally new aircraft; whilst Martin were asked to apply improvements to the

B-57 (a design built under licence by them, but actually developed by the English Electric Company and known in RAF service as the Canberra). In July 1953, six-month study contracts had been agreed with each company and the project, identified as MX-2147, was given the classified code name of 'Bald Eagle'.

Developments in camera and film technology, required to gather surveillance data from high altitude, had been proceeding in parallel with those made by the aerospace industry. Having established the Photographic Laboratory at Wright Field before the Second World War, Brig Gen George Goddard recruited two individuals, Cols Richard Philbrick and Amrom Katz, who continued in service after the war. Renamed the Aerial Reconnaissance Laboratory, Goddard also helped establish a group of optical research specialists that formed the Boston University Optical Research Centre. These included its director, Doctor Duncan MacDonald. In addition, there were notable industrialists and academics serving on various presidential panels who also played a key role in the development of high altitude reconnaissance imagery; people such as Harvard astronomer Doctor James Baker, Edwin Land, inventor of the Polaroid camera, Allen Donovan and Col Richard Leghorn, an airborne reconnaissance expert from Eastman Kodak. However, it was Jim Baker who had, by the end of WWII, produced the first 100-inch focal length precision lens for an aerial camera. This work was continued at Boston by Dunc MacDonald and his team in the early post-war years and culminated in a massive 240-inch focal length lens which, at fourteen feet, could only fit into an RB-36!

As US fears of a possible surprise Soviet ICBM attack continued to mount, the Air Force set up a study group at Boston to look further into the aerial reconnaissance

problem. Code named 'Beacon Hill', it was chaired by
Carl Overhage, and first assembled in May 1951.
Bringing together Baker, Land and Donovan, some of
this team also became members of the so-called Killian
committee, set up by President Eisenhower in 1954. It
served under James R Killian, and would drive the
decision to build a light-weight reconnaissance aircraft.

By January 1954, Bell, Fairchild and Martin had
completed their studies and submitted them to Wright
Field for evaluation. Apart from all three companies
nominating the new Pratt & Whitney J57 axial flow
turbojet engine (with high altitude modifications, the
full designation would become J57-P-37), the design
submissions varied considerably. As requested, Martin's
proposed Model 294 was a big wing version of the B-57;
Bell's Model 67 was a frail-looking twin-engined craft,
whilst the single-engined Fairchild M-195 featured an
over-the-fuselage intake and a stub-boom mounting for
vertical and horizontal tail surfaces.

By March 1954, engineers at Wright Field had
nominated Martin's B-57D as the interim design, whilst
the Bell proposal was felt to be the more suitable,
longer-term design. Consequently, a list of B-57
modifications was sent to Air Research and Development
Command (ARDC) Headquarters, to enable urgent Air
Force intelligence requirements in Europe to be met.

In April, Seaburg briefed all three designs to ARDC
and Strategic Air Command (SAC). This was followed a
month later by yet another briefing, this time to Air
Force Headquarters in Washington DC. Shortly
afterwards Seaburg received approval to proceed with
the B-57D and tentative approval for the Bell Model 67;
however, on 18th May an unsolicited proposal
originating from Lockheed hit his desk!

It was perhaps inevitable that someone in the Pentagon would leak details of the classified high-altitude reconnaissance proposal to Lockheed's Advanced Development Projects boss, aircraft design genius, Clarence L 'Kelly' Johnson. However, after a short but detailed review, Seaburg and his staff rejected the Lockheed design, designated CL-282, and in June 1954 Kelly received a letter officially rejecting his proposal. Undaunted, Kelly decided to pursue funding from alternative sources. Shortly afterwards he therefore presented a refined design submission to a Central Intelligence Agency (CIA) study committee.

With the Killian Committee having been briefed earlier on all four 'Bald Eagle' contenders and the CIA becoming increasingly enamoured of the idea of establishing its

Left When initially delivered to the Air Force, the U-2As were operated in natural metal finish and standard markings. (Lockheed Martin)

Middle left and bottom left Starting life as a U-2A, Article 393 was converted to a dual control U-2CT trainer in 1973. The elevated second cockpit was accommodated in what was formerly the Q-bay. (Paul Crickmore)

Right In the cramped confines of early U-2 cockpits, partial pressure suits were worn. Here NASA pilot Jim Hoyt undergoes a check in his S100 suit. (Paul Crickmore)

Below Unusually for a military aircraft of its size, the U-2's ailerons and elevators are controlled via a yoke. (Lockheed Martin)

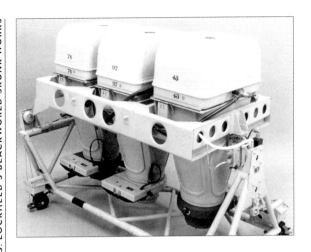

Above Type A system, three Hycon HR-73224 cameras.

Above The Itek Iris II Panoramic camera.

own airborne reconnaissance capability, Kelly met with the Government Advisory Board on 19 November 1954. During the course of that meeting he was told that he ... "was essentially being drafted for the project".

The Killian Committee's decision to back the refined CL-282 proposal was communicated to Secretary of Defence, Charles Wilson and CIA Director, Allen Dulles. They subsequently briefed President Eisenhower and sought authorisation for a programme to produce twenty aircraft at a total cost of $35 million. This was duly sanctioned.

A day later Dulles recruited Richard Bissell (a brilliant economist who lectured at both Yale and MIT), to manage the programme. That same day, Kelly received a phone call giving him the go-ahead for project 'Aquatone'. Within days, Lockheed's ADP office, better known as 'the Skunk Works', had by default become a full-scale, advanced design, engineering and production facility. The requirement for absolute secrecy meant that in the years ahead, the Skunk Works team were assured a high degree of autonomy from the rest of the Lockheed Corporation; additionally, the high level of specialised support required to run the programme, coupled with the lack of CIA expertise in this field, ensured Lockheed's participation in the programme for the life of the aircraft. With one decision, a series of precedents had been set for future aircraft programmes.

The Skunk Works had come into being back in 1943, following Lockheed's successful bid to build the United States first jet fighter. Kelly recruited the finest engineers from the Burbank facility and put them to work in an area isolated and secure from the rest of the plant - building the XP-80 in just 143 days! The high level of secrecy surrounding the facility's activities, together with its location - adjacent to the unit's awful-smelling, plastics manufacturing plant, caused Ervin Culver, a talented engineer on Kelly's team (who later invented the rigid rotor system for helicopters), to habitually answer the telephone using the name 'Skunk Works', after a location in a popular wartime comic strip, written by Al Capp - the name stuck.

The team Kelly recruited to design and build the new aircraft included Dick Boehme (project engineer), Art

Viereck (head of manufacturing), Ed Baldwin and some fifty other key engineers. Kelly nominated Tony LeVier (chief test pilot on the XF-104), to be the projects chief test pilot, but his first task was to find a secret site from which to conduct flight tests. After flying around for two weeks with Dorsey Kammerer, in Lockheed's V-tailed Beech Bonanza, Tony presented a short list of three possible sites to Kelly, who chose the one at the top of the list - Groom Lake. The site fell within the boundaries of the main Atomic Energy Commission (AEC) nuclear test site. Therefore the area had been cleared, fenced off and granted a restricted airspace zone. Within three months, under the auspices of Richard Bissell, a large team of AEC construction crews worked round the clock to transform the site into a basic test facility, consisting of a tarmac runway, two hangers and a number of accommodation trailers. An additional veil of secrecy was provided when it was agreed that all information released into the public domain would state that the aircraft had been developed as a high-altitude research tool, in service primarily with the National Advisory Committee for Aeronautics (NACA, later redesignated NASA).

To ensure that 'Kelly's Angel' (as the design was being referred to by some in the Skunk Works), maintained a competitive edge over its rival, the Bell 67 (now officially designated X-16 by the Air Force as a cover), Kelly promised that his design would be airborne in no more than eight months after the first metal was cut. The initial batch of twenty aircraft were built at the Burbank plant, thereafter further production was moved to Oildale, near Bakersfield, California. On 15 March 1955, wind tunnel testing of the design had been successfully completed and on 21 May, the fuselage of 'Article 341', the prototype, was removed from the jig. On 20 July, the completed aircraft was handed over to inspection for final checks. The next day it was disassembled and put into loading carts. At daybreak on 24 July, Article 341 was loaded into an Air Force C-124 and flown to Groom Lake, or Area 51. There it was reassembled in the semi-completed hangars and three days later static engine runs were initiated. With taxi tests completed - the third of which culminated in the aircraft inadvertently getting

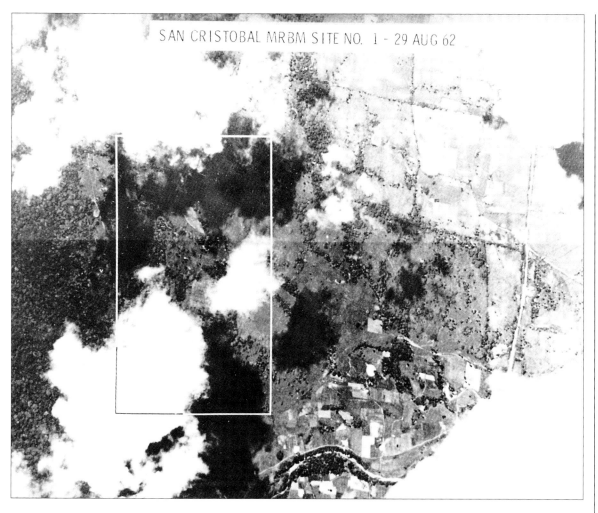

SAN CRISTOBAL MRBM SITE NO. 1 - 29 AUG 62

Above This is one of a series of shots taken by an 'Agency' U-2 overflight of Cuba on 29 August 1962, when concerns were raised that Soviet MRBMs had been deployed on the island. (CIA)

Below left and below right Surveillance of Cuba continued throughout the crisis, providing decision makers with vital information of the build-up and later deactivation of weapons systems. (CIA)

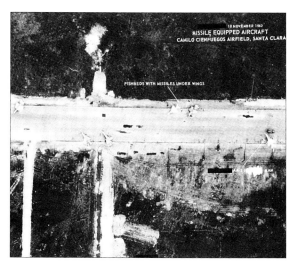

airborne, to a height of 35ft. The first scheduled flight took place at 15:55 hrs on 4 August 1955. Witnessed by several key Skunk Works and 'Agency' people, Tony LeVier, (using the call sign Angel 1), was chased by a Lockheed operated C-47, flown by company test pilot Bob Matye accompanied by Kelly Johnson (Matye would be the second pilot to fly the aircraft). Kelly had insisted that Tony should land the aircraft in a nose-level-main-gear-first attitude. However, after five attempts Tony abandoned this technique and landed the aircraft, having been airborne for 45 minutes, using a conventional tail-wheel-first landing.

It was during phase one of the flight test programme that the aircraft was officially designated U-2, the U for Utility, again designed to obscure the aircraft's true mission. Bell's X-16 had also been progressing well, with construction getting underway in September 1954 and its

Right The pledge given by President Eisenhower and repeated by Kennedy, that the US would conduct no more manned over-flights of Soviet territory following the Gary Powers shoot down, implicitly excluded other Communist Bloc countries and the People's Republic of China. In early 1959 the first of several cadres of Chinese Nationalist pilots arrived at Laughlin to begin U-2 flying training. From 1960 to 1968 these brave pilots conducted numerous overflights, gleaning vital intelligence relating to the Republic's emerging nuclear capability - several aircraft were shot down and put on display at the Peking People's Museum. (Paul Crickmore Collection)

Below In Late 1968, the U-2R entered service under the auspices of the Agency and was primarily employed in operations conducted by the Nationalist Chinese over the Republic of China. (Lockheed Martin)

first flight scheduled for early 1956. However, with the Agency, not the Air Force, now responsible for high-altitude reconnaissance, the X-16's raison d'etre had disappeared. Consequently, two months after the U-2 took to the air, a decision was made to terminate the X-16 contract - it was a bitter blow for Bell and one that had serious financial implications for several years.

The first of six RB-57s were delivered to SAC, under Project Black Knight, in March 1956. Operated by the 4080th Strategic Reconnaissance Wing (SRW), 4025th Strategic Reconnaissance Squadron (SRS), located at Turner AFB, Georgia, the unit conducted its first operational deployment, under Operation Sea Lion, just four months after activation. Most of these early operations were Electronic Intelligence/Signal Intelligence (ELINT/ SIGINT) missions, flown from Operating Locations (OLs), at Yokota AFB, Japan and, briefly, Eilson AFB, Alaska.

Highly classified, these ferret sorties utilised specialist equipment designated Model 320 or SAFE (Semi - Automatic Ferret Equipment), which had been tested during 1956 and 1957, under the Blue Tail Fly project; thereafter it was declared operational and deployed. In addition, the unit conducted high altitude sampling, during which particles were collected from the upper atmosphere, following nuclear tests undertaken by China and the Soviet Union. This enabled scientists to ascertain the weapons' characteristics: yield, efficiency etc.

In February 1957 the 4025th relocated from Turner to Laughlin AFB, Texas and one month later they received the last of twenty RB-57Ds ordered by the Air Force. For six month,s further air sampling flights were conducted, this time from Eniwetok Proving Grounds, on the Marshall Islands. Then, in early 1959, under Operation Bordertown, the unit deployed to Europe, where they continued to conduct air sampling and ELINT/SIGINT missions, before returning to Laughlin and deactivating in mid-1959.

Back at Area 51, Tony LeVier had completed a total of twenty flights in the U-2 and on 1 September, he left Project Aquatone, having been promoted to Director of Flying, back at Burbank. Planning flight tests became the responsibility of Ernie Joiner and these were now flown by test pilots Bob Matye and Ray Goadey.

Technical Overview

The original CL-282 design submission consisted of a slightly modified XF-104 Starfighter fuselage and tail assembly, a large span high aspect ratio wing and a General Electric J73 - GE-3 non-afterburning turbo jet. However, the J73 was an unknown (and in the long run

Above Bill Park carrier-qualified the U-2R aboard *USS America* (CVA-66) in 1969. A similar exercise had taken place in early 1964, when Bob Schumacher qualified a modified U-2, redesignated U-2G, aboard *USS Ranger* (CVA-63). (Lockheed Martin)

Left One-third larger than the earlier U-2A/C versions, the U-2R brought with it major improvements in mission capability, payload capability, range and crew comfort. (Lockheed Martin)

Below Operated by NASA as an ER-2 (Earth Resources), serial 708, this aircraft began life as TR-1 serial 80-1069. Apparent is the more commodious cockpit. (Paul Crickmore)

unsuccessful) power plant. Acceptance of the CL–282 design concept became conditional upon it being powered by the J-57. During this enforced redesign, the fuselage was both lengthened and widened to accommodate the new engine. The F-104 'T' tail was replaced by a conventional unit and the cockpit pressurised.

To achieve the required operating altitudes, the design was aerodynamically clean and the quest for weight reduction almost obsessive – the aircraft's unladen weight being just 12,000 lbs. Conventional flight control surfaces on the U-2 consisted of ailerons with a travel of 16 degrees up and 14 degrees down; elevator that travelled 30 degrees up and 20 down and a rudder that deflected 30 degrees left and right. Due to wing flex, the flaps are segmented into four sections on each wing and are actuated to a maximum of 35 degrees down by two hydraulic motors, interconnected by a flexible synchronisation shaft. Integral with the flap system is the U-2's unique gust control system, this enables both ailerons to move 10 degrees and the flaps 4 degrees simultaneously when flying through turbulent air or when cruising at higher speeds in smooth air.

The U-2A's single Pratt & Whitney J57-P-37 non afterburning turbojet produced 10,500 lbs of thrust at take off and 8,100 lbs at normal cruise. This axial flow, dual compressor unit featured a nine-stage low pressure assembly followed by a seven-stage high pressure unit. Air was then supplied to the can annular combustion chamber, where a special low vapour pressure kerosene, developed by Shell Oil, designated LF-1A by Lockheed and JP-TS (for Thermally Stable) by the military, was ignited in eight burner cans (two spark igniters were located in cans 4 & 5 and ignition in the remaining cans was achieved utilising connecting flame tubes). The gas stream then entered the turbine section, the first stage being used to drive the high pressure compressor via a hollow shaft; the second and third turbine stages driving the low pressure compressor via a concentric shaft located through the hollow, high pressure compressor shaft. A gear box, driven off the high pressure compressor shaft, provided power for the starter, tachometer, fuel pump and fuel control unit. The turbine high velocity gases were then discharged through a fixed area exhaust nozzle.

As payload weights increased, in 1958 it was decided to uprate the U-2's propulsion system to the Pratt & Whitney J75. The two variants of this engine, the J75-P-13A and the later J75-P-13B, increased available take-off thrust to 15,800 lbs and then to 17,000 lbs, for normal cruise thrust this increased to 13,900 lbs, then to 15,100 lbs respectively.

The U-2 has both an AC and a DC electrical system. The AC system is provided by a 750-VA inverter for normal operation with an additional 750-VA inverter as back up. In emergencies a 100-VA inverter and a 10-KVA engine driven AC generator are provided. DC power is produced by one 400 amp, 28 volt, engine-driven generator. A 35 amp/hour, nickel cadmium battery provides emergency DC power. Should the main generator fail in late-build aircraft, a single AC/DC generator, backed up by an AC alternator driven from the hydraulic system, provides power to all essential equipment. The hydraulic system is a constant 3,000 psi pressure type, incorporating an accumulator and self-regulating engine-driven pump. The air-charged accumulator stores pressures for peak demands, thus reducing fluctuations in pump loading. It operates the landing gear, speed brakes, wing flaps, fuel boost pump drive motor; and on the U-2F, the latch reciprocal mechanism on the air refuelling system (on late model aircraft this system also operates the pitch trim and spoilers).

Retracting forward, the titanium, zero track landing gear, is of bicycle layout, consisting of twin main and tail wheels. Pogos, or outriggers, are located under each wing at about mid-semi-span, to provide support during ground handling; these too, have twin tyres and are gravity-pull-jettisoned, shortly after the wings begin to generate lift. The main gear tyres are conventional high

Below With the advent of the TR-1/U-2R, pilots were at last able to wear full-pressure suits. This is the David Clark Company's S1031 suit. (Lockheed Martin)

pressure units, however, both the Pogo tyres and those of the tail wheel are of solid rubber construction, requiring no inflation. Ground steering is achieved using the rudder pedals, which are interconnected by cables to the tail wheel.

The size of the U-2's cockpit, varies significantly with variant, however, the general layout is common to all types. Perhaps the two most immediate features upon entering the cockpit are the aircraft's control yoke (which looks as if it was stolen off the C-130 production line) and the Baird Scientific drift sight, which dominates the upper centre of the front instrumental panel. Utilising a system of mirrors and prisms, the drift sight, with its 360

Above U-2R 80-1067 lines up at Palmdale. (Lockheed Martin)

Below As the long wings get airborne, the pogos or outrigger wheels, are detached and recovered by ground support staff. (Lockheed Martin)

degree, horizon to horizon scanning head, enables the pilot to visually check the aircraft's ground track. A rubber cone attached to the display eliminates stray light when viewing the scope. The cockpit is pressurised to maintain an equivalent pressure altitude of 28,000ft. Although the aircraft was initially flown without ejector seats, all aircraft were later re-configured to accommodate a limited capability Lockheed-developed seat, which utilises a 'low-g' catapult to minimise compression injuries.

In earlier model U-2s, the mission payload was located in a cavernous, pressurised area, behind the cockpit, known as the Q-bay. As previously mentioned, the acquisition of photographic intelligence (PHOTINT), was to be the aircraft's primary mission. Dr Jim Baker proved to be pivotal in the conceptualisation of the camera system deployed for the U-2. Three camera systems were worked up; the Type A, was primarily refurbished Air Force stock and a stop-gap. The type C, with its 180 inch focal length lens, would be overtaken by events. However, the Type B camera would prove to be Project Aquatone's workhorse. Optimising a 36-inch focal length lens, its large format film (18 x18 in) was loaded on to two 6,500 foot rolls. When the system was activated, the camera imaged onto two 9.5-inch wide frames, through a single lens, thereby providing very high resolution, stereo coverage of the collection area with a 50-70% overlap. Manufactured by the Hycon Corporation, the Type B camera system weighed about 500 lbs, including film. Also located in the Q bay was a 35mm tracker camera. This scanned from horizon to horizon throughout the flight, thereby providing the photographic interpreters with an accurate ground track of the aircraft's flight path.

Operations

All Agency pilots recruited into Project Aquatone came straight from the Air Force, on a 'suspended contract', in which their 'grey suit' time counted towards their time served in the military. Two of the initial cadre of six pilots, Marty Knutson and Carmen Vito, were both F-84 'jocks', assigned to the 31st Strategic Fighter Wing, locat-

ed at Turner AFB, Georgia. Having passed various interviews, conducted by mysterious civilians at insalubrious hotels, they next spent a week undergoing one of the most rigorous medicals ever devised, at the Lovelace Clinic, Alburquerque, New Mexico. In all, about 25 pilots, in three intakes, would be recruited into the Agency programme.

Early U-2 training flights were punctuated by a number of flameouts, a situation that continued until Pratt & Whitney engineers perfected high altitude operation of the J57. Such events required the pilot to seek out denser air at 35,000 feet, in order to effect a relight. On a few occasions, when pilots were unable to get a relight, it became necessary to divert. But despite a number of such occurrences, Aquatone remained in the black.

A unique facet of U-2 piloting, was flight in that part of the envelope known as 'coffin corner'. Having climbed rapidly to 60,000 feet the aircraft would then follow a cruise–climb schedule; as fuel was burned off and the aircraft became lighter, it could climb higher - as high as

Top left NACA/NASA association with the U-2 can be traced back to the beginning of the programme. Initially a CIA paper exercise, designed to cover the aircraft's true mission, NASA received two U-2Cs (56-6681 and 56-6682 redesignated NASA 708 and 709 respectively), on the 3rd and 4th June 1971, to form its High Altitude Missions Branch (HAMB), based at Moffett Field, California. (Paul Crickmore)

Top right When U-2C 56-6681 was retired in June 1987, its NASA designation, 708, was transferred to an ex- Air Force TR-1 (80-1069), which served alongside the purpose-built ER-2 prototype NASA 706 and the remaining U-2C, NASA 709. (Paul Crickmore)

Above NASA U-2C 709 was retired in April 1989 and at the time of writing, following delivery of the second ER-2, NASA 709, the fleet consists of two ER-2s (now redesignated U-2ERs) and the ex-Air Force TR-1 (U-2R). (Lockheed Martin)

75,000 feet in some flight conditions. However, in the rarefied air above 60,000 feet, the never exceed speed curve virtually meets the aircraft stall speed curve. This crucial difference could be as little as 10kts. At high altitude with the engine at full power and in a banked turn, it was possible for the high wing to reach Mach buffet whilst the inside wing approached stall buffet – exceed Mach buffet by more than four knots and it was possible that the fragile U-2 would disintegrate!

During the Geneva Summit, on 21 July 1955, President Eisenhower had proposed that an 'Open Skies' plan should be considered between the United States, the Soviet Union and other participating countries, wherein a limited number of annual reconnaissance overflights would be made in order to verify claims of declared force strengths. Surprised by the proposal, the Soviet delega-tion reacted favourably and agreed to confer with their Party Secretary, Nikita Khrushchev. He however refused to either sign-up to, or reject the proposal. Such prevari-cation ensured that 'Open Skies' failed one month later, when a vote was taken in the United Nations.

By June 1956, it was judged that initial flight test and

Above left Unique to U-2 operations is the 'howdah', which was designed to protect crew members from the sun's heat. (Lockheed Martin)

Below U-2R, 80-1082 equipped with short nose but super-pods is seen complete with tail-art at Beale AFB in November 1986. (Paul Crickmore)

Above Slow sink rate, due to the high aspect ratio wing, has always caused problems when landing U-2s; as a result, every landing - including touch-and-goes, are accompanied by two 'mobile' U-2 pilots, one in radio contact, in a fast car. As the U-2 crosses the threshold it is chased and height-to-go is called-off. (Paul Crickmore)

Right Airborne in just over 1,000ft of runway, the U-2's climb rate has always been impressive; with lighter, earlier models reaching 50,000ft in just 10 minutes. (Paul Crickmore)

training objectives of the U-2 programme had been completed; accordingly six operational pilots, together with ten U-2s, were deemed ready for operational deployment. The death of Eisenhower's 'Open Skies' proposal led the President to sanction, for an initial ten-day period, a program that would have a profound impact within the intelligence fraternity and on international power politics - Operation Overflight. In anticipation of these events, two U-2s had been air-freighted to RAF Lakenheath, England on 30 April 1956, where the first of three Agency detachments was formed, under the entirely fictional designation of 1st Weather Reconnaissance Squadron, Provisional (WRSP-1). Known within the

'inner circle' as 'Detachment A' and consisting of Agency, Air Force and contracted civilians, no operational sorties were flown from the UK and the unit redeployed to Wiesbaden, Germany on 15 June. This new location was situated close to Camp King, the Agency's main West German intelligence gathering facility, within which intel reports from defectors were collected and then used as a basis for U-2 overflight requests.

The first operational U-2 sortie was flown just four days after Det A's arrival at Wiesbaden. Piloted by Carl Overstreet, the platform overflew Warsaw, Berlin and Potsdam, before recovering back into Wiesbaden without incident. Image quality provided by the Type B camera surpassed anything previously seen, and the stage was set for 'Overflight' to begin operations against the Soviet Union. This was achieved by Hervey Stockman, flying Article 347 on US Independence Day, 4 July 1956. He flew over East Berlin then across northern Poland via Poznan, onward to Minsk and Leningrad, before exiting via the Baltic states of Estonia, Latvia and Lithuania, landing again without incident back at Wiesbaden after a flight lasting eight hours 45 minutes.

The very next day Article 347 was again airborne, this time with Carmen Vito at the controls on an overflight which included the Soviet capital, Moscow. Again, image quality was exceptional, but on this occasion Soviet fighters tried, unsuccessfully, to intercept the flight. Yet another mission was successfully completed the following Monday, by which time the Soviet 'diplomatic cage' was well and truly rattled. On 10 July the Soviet Ambassador in Washington delivered a formal, public protest against the flights. Eisenhower was very concerned at the level of provocation that these flights inevitably caused and insisted that henceforth, ten-day blanket clearances were rescinded, and instead replaced by a policy of one clearance, one flight.

The imagery secured by these first sorties was developed and duplicated at Wiesbaden, before one set was despatched by special courier aircraft to Washington (the other set was retained at Wiesbaden in case the first was lost or damaged in transit). Once in Washington, they ended up in a run-down neighbourhood where Art Lundahl, of the Agency's Photographic Intelligence Division, had set up a secret process and interpretation centre, on the upper floors of an auto repair shop, aptly codenamed 'Auto Mat'.

The vast amount of quality imagery collected by 'Overflight' soon put the Agency at odds with gloomy Air Force predictions about the strength of the Soviet bomber fleet, which forced a downward reappraisal of a National Intelligence Estimate (NIE). One disturbing aspect revealed by the flights however was the ease with which Soviet radar was able to track them with early warning and height finding radars. This in turn led the Skunk Works to undertake a series of evaluations using various techniques to reduce the U-2's Radar Cross Section (RCS). Utilising Article 341 up at Area 51, Project Dirty Bird first saw the aircraft's planform framed by wires of different dipole lengths running from tail to wing. Another used Radar Absorbent Material (RAM), in the

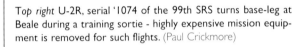

Top right U-2R, serial '1074 of the 99th SRS turns base-leg at Beale during a training sortie - highly expensive mission equipment is removed for such flights. (Paul Crickmore)

Right 1082 taxies to a halt on completion of a low altitude training sortie. Note the externally mounted rear-view mirror, located on the left side of the cockpit canopy. (Paul Crickmore)

Below On 2 August 1988, General Rogers, then Commander-in-Chief of Strategic Air Command, experienced at first hand a high altitude familiarization flight in a TR-1B. (Paul Crickmore)

form of a metallic grid, known as a Salisbury Screen. Attached to 341's lower surfaces, this was then covered in 'Echosorb' - a microwave-absorbent coating based on black rubber foam; but neither technique proved effective.

It was during a Dirty Bird test flight on 4 April 1957, that Article 341, the U-2 prototype, was lost. Having suffered a flame out at about 72,000 feet, Bob Sieker's pressure suit inflated, unfortunately the clasp securing the bottom of his face plate failed. With 70 lbs of internal pressure exhausting through the front of the helmet, it would have been almost impossible for Bob to resecure the clasp and within ten seconds he lost consciousness. Article 341 descended in a flat spin, and upon reaching denser air, it appears that Bob revived and attempted a bail out. The aircraft's wreckage remained more or less in one piece and was eventually found about ninety miles from Area 51. Bob's body was recovered about fifty feet away, suggesting he may have managed to clear the aircraft just before impact. Kelly Johnson redesigned the face plate clasp and re-evaluated the decision not to equip U-2s with an ejector seat - had this aircraft been so equipped, it is probable that Bob would have survived.

In August 1956, the second cadre of Agency pilots had completed their training up at Area 51 and were shipped to Incirlik AB, Turkey, where they formed 'Detachment B', which consisted of seven pilots and five aircraft. A third U-2 operating location - Det C, was established at Atsugi airfield near Tokyo in 1957 and in February that same year, the last Agency pilots graduated and were dispersed to the three Dets. By now Det A had again moved, this time to Giebelstadt, just south of Wurzburg and shortly afterwards it was merged with Det B. As the 1950s drew to a close, Agency U-2s had successfully completed about thirty overflights of the Soviet Union and considerably more peripheral and training missions.

From its inception, Lockheed, the Agency and DoD officials all believed that the U-2's overflight life would last about two years. But as year three drew to a close, there still appeared to be a gap between the U-2's ability to overfly denied territory and the Soviet's to build a weapons system capable of successfully intercepting the intruder. Certainly the program's accomplishments were approaching legendary status; in addition to revealing the truth about the Soviet bomber fleet, it had, while operating out of Lahore and Peshawar, Pakistan, discovered the location of a new ICBM (Intercontinental Ballistic Missile), test site at Tyuratam, which turned out to be the primary test facility for the new R-7 ICBM (later known by NATO as the SS-6 Sapwood).

The potential threat represented by the Soviet's SA-2

Below A high accident rate during flight training led to two U-2As being converted into U-2CT configuration. These were both retired and replaced by three TR-1Bs. (Paul Crickmore)

Bottom With the instructor pilot (IP) seated in the raised rear cockpit, a student brings 1065 over the Beale threshold. Ten feet 'off the deck' and 200 feet in the overrun, with a 10kt head-wind, the throttle is brought to idle and the aircraft 'driven down' to just one or two feet, where it is held until it stalls. (Paul Crickmore)

Above Not long after their arrival at Beale, the white training birds were painted black. Later their designation was changed from TR-1Bs to U-2RTs. When re-engined with the F118, they became U-2 STs; and finally today they are designated TU-2Ss. (Paul Crickmore)

Right Designed to fit on an aircraft carrier's elevator, the outer 6 feet of a U-2R's wing folds inboard. (Paul Crickmore)

Guideline, surface to air missile (SAM) system, touting a kill pattern of about 400 feet, was certainly appreciated by U-2 mission planners, who gave known sites a berth of up to 30 miles. Further precautions saw the introduction of a rudimentary Electronic Countermeasure (ECM) suite. Designated System 9, this simple range gate pull-off (RGPO) device, was located in a small aft-facing compartment at the root of the vertical fin. Switched on by the pilot upon entering denied territory, it had the capability of breaking lock if illuminated by an airborne intercept radar. Additional comfort came from the first major U-2 upgrade which had just been initiated; five aircraft were reworked into U-2C models, powered by an uprated Pratt & Whitney J75 engine, which enabled the aircraft to climb an additional 5,000 feet.

On the diplomatic stage a visit by Khrushchev to the United States prompted a reciprocal invitation for Eisenhower to visit the Soviet Union during 1960. In the meantime, it was agreed a summit would be held in Paris, to which both the British and French would be invited. A thaw in the frosty relationship between the two super powers seemed in prospect. However, all this was about to change.

Mayday

One of the most ambitious sorties planned for the U-2 was a nine hour flight covering 3,800 miles (2,900 of which would be over denied territory). Launched from Peshawar, Pakistan, the flight would recover into Bodo, Norway. The mission's objective was to locate a new missile base near Plestsk that the photo interpreters at Auto Mat had been searching for in vain since 1958. In addition, the route offered an opportunity of gaining additional material from Tyuratam and the military industrial complex around Sverdlovrk.

Above The U-2R still retains the early high altitude air sampling capability; here the unit is being bolted into 69-10338's Q-bay. (Paul Crickmore)

Right Nose-art, or in this case, tail-art, has been a feature of US combat aircraft since WWII. This particular example, applied in chalk, adorned the tail of a TR-1B. (Paul Crickmore)

The plan was reluctantly approved by President Eisenhower, who insisted that it should be flown before 25 April. However, due to bad weather across much of the intended route, Eisenhower agreed to extend the deadline to 1 May. On Wednesday 27 April, improving met conditions prompted a detachment from Det B consisting of two pilots and support personnel to deploy via C-130 from Incirlik, to Peshawar. Scheduled attempts to launch on 28, 29 and 30 April were made. However,

all were aborted well before take-off, due to adverse weather in the collection areas. Finally, at 06:26 local time, on May 1 1960, Francis Gary Powers got airborne in Article 360 and headed for the border. To help draw attention away from the deep penetration mission, a diversionary, peripheral flight left from Incirlik. After three hours and 27 minutes of flight, Powers was stunned to feel and hear what seemed to be a dull explosion, below and behind his aircraft. Almost immediately

afterwards the sky turned bright orange and seconds later 360's right wing dropped. Turning the control yoke left, Powers managed to correct the roll, but then the nose pitched downward - due to damage sustained by the horizontal tail. As the U-2 pitched violently forward, both wings were ripped from the fuselage. Powers face plate frosted over, his partial pressure suite inflated and what was left of the aircraft entered an inverted flat spin. Centrifugal forces pinned the pilot to the instrument

Above The 17th Reconnaissance Wing and its flying component, the 95th Reconnaissance Squadron, were activated at RAF Alconbury on 1 October 1982 and became operational five months later. (Paul Crickmore)

Right Steve Nichols lines-up 'KONA 17' an ASARS configured aircraft, prior to departure from Alconbury. (Paul Crickmore)

panel which prevented the use of the ejector seat. Glancing at the unwinding altimeter, Powers noted he was descending through 34,000 ft. Reaching up he pushed the canopy open, unlatched his seat harness and was thrown forward. Now only half out of the cockpit, he realised he'd failed to disconnect his oxygen hose. He then attempted to re-enter the cockpit. When this failed, he began pulling on the hose in an effort to break it. Finally his efforts were rewarded and he was clear; almost immediately his chute was successfully deployed by a barometric sensor - set to activate at 15,000ft. Powers was captured after landing in a field and four days later the political impact of the shoot down reverberated across the front pages of newspapers all around the world. Operation Overflight, the United States' most clandestine reconnaissance operation, had literally been blown apart at the seams. An immediate cessation of U-2 overflights followed, backed up later by the retraction of all U-2 operations around the world.

On 10 February 1962 Frank Powers and the notorious master spy, Rudolf Abel silently passed one another on the Glienicker Bridge in Germany, in a pre-arranged exchange of prisoners. But with 90% of all photographic data on Soviet military developments originating from U-2 imagery, the question remained: how, or with what, would it be replaced?

Air Force Operations

With the Agency U-2 operation up and running, the Air Force began recruiting pilots for its program largely from the same source; namely, the two recently deactivated SAC F-84 wings at Turner AFB, Georgia. Having undertaken ground crew and pilot training at Area 51, Col Jack Nole, commander of the 4028 Strategic Reconnaissance Squadron (SRS), led the first of two three-ship U-2 formations down to their new home at Laughlin AFB, Texas on 11 June 1957. Part of the 4080 SRW, their

sister squadron, the 4025th SRS, were equipped with Martin RB-57Ds. Seventeen days later disaster struck. Shortly before 9am on Friday 28 June, Lt Ford Lowcock crashed his U-2 near Del Rio, a few miles from Laughlin, and was killed, just three days after his first U-2 flight. Then, three hours later, Lt Leo Smith crashed his U-2 about thirty miles north of Abilene, Texas. He too was killed. Accident investigations determined that fuel imbalance in the wing tanks was probably a contributory factor in both incidents.

During September, the 4028th received five more U-2s which were assigned to the Air Force project HASP (High Altitude Sampling Program), sponsored by the Defence Atomic Support Agency (DASA). The objective was to determine the role played by the stratosphere in the worldwide distribution of fusion products resulting from nuclear explosions. In all the program lasted five years and involved some 45,000 flying hours - almost all in U-2s. Eventually DASA published its results, making its findings available to the UN. The result was a ban on all 'air burst' testing of nuclear weapons.

To the Brink

During July and August 1962, John McCone, Director of the 'Agency' (he replaced Allen Dulles after the CIA-sponsored 'Bay of Pigs' affair), received a number of increasingly disturbing accounts concerning a Soviet military build-up on the island of Cuba. On 22 August he went directly to President Kennedy stating that it was his belief that Cuba were receiving intermediate range

Below left During the 'bad old days' of the Cold War, Alconbury based aircraft would usually take up station over Germany, reaching 60,000ft about 30 miles south of Amsterdam, whereupon they would turn off their mode 'Charlie' height read-out. (Paul Crickmore)

Below The 95RS used ROOK as its call sign for all training sorties. Here Maj Blaire Bachus, flying '093, Rook 32, climbs away after another touch and go. (Paul Crickmore)

ballistic missiles. The President demanded corroborative evidence of such aggression before taking further action. Consequently, CIA U-2 overflights of the island were stepped up, with flights on the 28th August, 5, 17, 26 and 29 September and the 5 and 7 October. However, only evidence of SAM construction sites and increased fighter activity including the delivery of MiG-21s was detected. It was an alert photo-interpreter in the Defence Intelligence Agency (DIA), who noticed that the layout of some of these SA-2 sites on Cuba matched those deployed to protect offensive ballistic missile sites in the Soviet Union. When the Committee on Overhead Reconnaissance (COMOR) reconvened on 4 October, further coverage of western Cuba was requested. Despite the risks, again it was decided to use the U-2. However, as a potential military conflict seemed to be brewing on the island, the Air Force, with support from the Secretary of Defence, Robert McNamara, insisted that it should fly all future U-2 sorties over Cuba. A view which, after some squabbling, was upheld, and on Wednesday 10 October the President sanctioned a resumption on U-2 flights over western Cuba.

It had been agreed that Agency U-2Cs would be used by the Air Force, as these were equipped with both System 9 and System 12 ECM units - the latter was a Radar Homing and Warning Receiver (RHAW), which warned the pilot if he was being tracked by SAM radars.

Majors Anderson and Heyser were chosen to conduct the flights as they had both checked out in the 'C' model, so they were packed off to Edwards North Base to join up with their mounts. Early on the morning of 14 October, Steve Heyser took off from Edwards and headed towards Isla de Pinos and then north toward the Cuban mainland. The most critical portion of the mission was the run from San Cristobal, which lasted approximately five minutes, after which Heyser set course for McCoy AFB, Florida - from where it had been agreed, future sorties over the island would be based. Upon landing, the

film was rushed to the National Photographic Interpretation Centre (NPIC), at Washington via a waiting Air Force jet. At about 5.30 on the afternoon of the 15th, Arthur Lundahl, the head of NPIC, passed the news to CIA headquarters - now located in Langley, Virginia - that Heysey's film had captured the required evidence. Khrushchev was in the process of deploying SS-4 MRBM's (NATO codename Scandal), right in America's back yard. Shortly before 9am on Tuesday the 16th, McGeorge Bundy, Kennedy's assistant for National Security Affairs, showed his president the photos. For the next thirteen days, Kennedy and a circle of his closest advisors became embroiled in a crisis that took the world to the brink of a nuclear holocaust.

Early on the morning of 15 October, Randy Anderson had launched from Edwards and conducted a sortie similar to that of Heyser, but it was appreciated that two U-2Cs would not be nearly enough resource for the job in hand. With its U-2s participating in the HASP and therefore stationed all around the globe, the 4028th SRS faced the challenge of gathering together enough aircraft to provide national command authorities with the vast amount of timely imagery upon which crucial decisions would be based. However, with extraordinary effort, the Air Force managed to muster ten aircraft and eleven pilots. At 4am on Tuesday 16th, three U-2 As were launched in blinding rain from Laughlin to conduct further overflights - like the preceding U-2Cs, they also recovered into McCoy.

As analysis of U-2 imagery continued, NPIC were able to confirm two MRBM sites near San Cristobal, each equipped with a regiment of eight SS-4s on launches with eight more ready for a second salvo, and that both sites were operational. Another regiment of SS-4s was discovered near Sagua La Grande; they were expected to become operational within a week. Finally the interpreters were convinced that they had also found two sites, near Guanajay, that were intended for the 2,200 mile-range

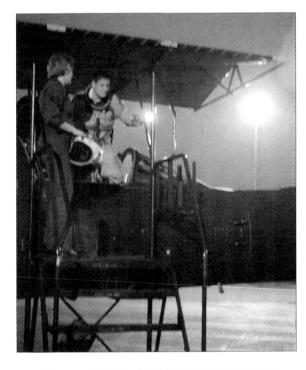

Top and above The original plans for the 17RW involved basing 12 aircraft at Alconbury and six at Weathersfield, two TR-1s were then to orbit over Central Europe 24 hours a day. In the event, Alconbury never operated more than eleven aircraft before the Cold War melted away. (Paul Crickmore Collection)

Right Returning from the Gulf War, these six U-2Rs were dispatched to Plant 2 at Palmdale, where Lockheed Martin provides support. (Lockheed Martin)

SS-5s (Skean), which, they predicted, would be operational in six to eight weeks - these missiles touted a range capability that threatened US ICBM bases in the north of the country. On top of all this, 4028th surveillance also discovered crates containing Ilyushin Il-28 bombers at San Julian airfield and thirty nine MiG-21s at Santa Clara.

In the cabinet room at 9.45 on Friday 19th October, Kennedy met with his joint Chiefs of Staff. The ever bullish Air Force Chief of Staff, Gen Curtis Le May, was in no doubt what should be done, ... " take out the missiles, I think you've got to take out their air with it, and their radar, communication, the whole works. It just doesn't make any sense to do anything but that."

Luckily for humanity, the result of a long-running meeting at the State Department on Saturday formed the basis of a more rational policy, which was accepted by Kennedy on Monday; namely, that the island would be blockaded and the United States would pledge to Khrushchev the withdrawal of US Jupiter IRBMs in Turkey, in exchange for a quid pro quo withdrawal of Soviet missiles in Cuba.

That same day, following further meetings with the JCS and briefings to Senior Democrat and Republican leaders of Congress, Kennedy delivered a televised address to tens of millions of anxious viewers across the United States, the speech was then re-broadcast and distributed in many languages around the world.

Now the crisis was in the public domain, low-level photo recce sorties by Air Force RF-101 Voodoos and US Navy RF-8 Crusaders were also authorised. On Wednesday 24th October, the first signs that sense was beginning to prevail emerged when Soviet freighters, en route to Cuba, were seen to heave to in mid Atlantic.

Three days later, Randy Anderson got airborne from McCoy in Article 343 for another overflight. Flying along the northern coast of Cuba, despite carrying the System 12 SAM radar warning receiver, he was taken by surprise by a salvo of SA-2s fired from Banes naval base, at the eastern end of the island. One missile exploded above and behind the aircraft.

Shrapnel penetrated the cockpit and Anderson's pressure suit. It is believed he was killed when the cockpit depressurised and his suit failed to inflate.

Less than a day after the loss of Major Anderson, Khrushchev announced on Moscow Radio that the Cuban missiles would be withdrawn, thus bringing to an end the most serious east/west standoff of the twentieth century.

Having moved from Laughlin to Davies-Monthan AFB, Arizona on 12 July 1963, the 4028th SRS compliment of reconnaissance gathering platforms increased substantially when an international agreement was reached to discontinue all above ground nuclear weapons testing and all HASP aircraft were re-configured accordingly.

31 December 1963 saw the beginning of another U-2 chapter when President Johnson granted his approval for its deployment to South Vietnam, under the SAC code name Dragon Lady. And so on 14 February 1964, four aircraft touched down at Bien Hoa, near Saigon, thus creating the detachment known as OL-20. Their mission was to provide covert surveillance of North Vietnam's border areas, particularly Vietcong infiltration routes and develop a contingency list of targets inside 'the North' should the war escalate - how prophetic such planning would prove to be …

Senior Year

By the middle of 1963 only 21 out of the original 55 U-2's remained, most having been lost over the years to various accidents. Mindful of the U-2's performance degradation, brought about by heavier payloads and the inability of engine improvements to compensate, Kelly Johnson embarked upon an investigation into ways of re-establishing the aircraft's performance. These began on 2 February 1965 and were referred to variously as the WU-2C or U-2N; in-house however, they were known as the CL-351. The emerging aircraft was one third larger than its predecessors and eventually became the U-2R. On 19 September 1966, the Air Force approved the construction of eight aircraft, placing a further order for four additional U-2Rs, four months later.
Final assembly took place in Building 309/310 at Burbank, after which Article 051 (the prototype) was trucked to Edwards North Base, for its first flight, an event that took place on 28 August 1967 - at the controls was Lockheed Test Pilot, Bill Park.

By February 1968, the second U-2R was dispatched to North Base, where it was received by a CIA unit designated Det G. By December 1968, all twelve aircraft had been delivered and equally split between the 'Agency' and the Air Force. In keeping with other Air Force projects, the 'Senior' codename given to the U-2R programme was Senior Year.

Throughout the 1970s, U-2Rs were put to work monitoring the Middle East and Cuba. In Southeast Asia,

Above and below Following extensive flight testing the P&W J75 engine has at last been replaced on the U-2 fleet by the General Electric F118-GE-101. All aircraft have accordingly been redesignated U-2S. The new engine is 1,300 lbs lighter and 16 per cent more fuel efficient, enabling the aircraft to gain another 3,500 ft in altitude and increase its range by 1,220n miles (or alternatively increase its boiler time). (Lockheed Martin)

OL-20 moved in July 1970 from Bien Hoa to U-Tapao, Thailand. Here a Melpur Commit sensor and datalink from the Sperry company was integrated into a U-2R, giving rise to the Senior Book, SigInt programme. These missions were flown mainly at night in racetrack orbits high above the Gulf of Tonkin, from where the U-2 eavesdropped on Vietnamese national and air defence communications, transmitting the data, in real time, to a ground station at Nakhon, Phanom, on the Thai border. These flights provided simultaneous communication relay facilities to other US aircraft in the region. By January 1973, operations increased to round-the-clock and OL-20 was redesignated the 99th SRS. SigInt coverage continued to improve and expand, giving rise to Senior Spear - this entailed antennas being moved from the fuselage into specially adapted pods faired into the wing. Then came Senior Stretch, where sigInt data collected by the U-2 was relayed from the ground station up to satellites and onward to the National Security Agency (NSA), Maryland. As the war in Vietnam drew to a close, followed by the inevitable cuts in defence spending, U-2s of the 100 SRW were, in July 1976, consolidated into the 1 SRW, at Beale AFB, California.

In August 1976, U-2R 68-10336 deployed to RAF Mildenhall, sporting two super pods. The pods housed spiral antennas for Elint collection, in a programme code-named Senior Ruby. As the decade drew to a close, the growing disparity between the size of Soviet and NATO conventional forces in Europe worried many western political and military leaders. It was thought that little could be done on a conventional battlefield to halt a Blitzkrieg type of attack carried out by the Warsaw Pact. The only counter to this would be a NATO pre-emptive strike, directed at such forces as they massed for attack. But this would require accurate all weather surveillance, extending well beyond the East-West border, which could then be made available to field commanders in near-real time. The hi-tech answer was to co-locate a system called Precision Location Strike System (PLSS), which identi-fied air defence radar and communications sites by homing in on their emissions, with a long-range, high resolution radar, being developed by Hughes, known as ASARS-2 - Advanced Synthetic Aperture Radar System (ASARS-1 was deployed on the SR-71). All of this digitised information could then be downloaded as required. With its additional capacity, high-altitude capability and proven long loiter time, the U-2R was the natural platform choice in which to site all of these 'black boxes'. Furthermore, in a move designed to shake off the 'spy-plane' tag once and for all, it was agreed that the aircraft would be renamed the TR-1, for Tactical Reconnaissance. But as Kelly Johnson's successor, Ben Rich, later remarked, "The press simply called it the TR-1 spyplane instead!".

Twenty-five TR-1s were ordered in the FY 1979 budget, at a cost of about $550 million, including sensors and ground support equipment. In addition, a further ten aircraft were ordered 'in the black', these would retain their U-2R designation and supplement those surviving from the earlier build.

The first Air Force TR-1, 80-1066, was publicly rolled out at site 7, Palmdale, on 15 July 1981 and was flown for the first time by Lockheed Test Pilot Ken Weir on 1 August. In-flight development of ASARS-2 had been conducted utilising U-2R, 68-10336 and early test results were remarkable.

Precision Location Strike System operation required three TR-1s to operate as a team. Loitering at high altitude with Elint sensors which were data-linked to a ground station they enabled threat emitters to be

Below The U-2R/S together with the RC-135 (depicted is an RC-135U, Combat Sent aircraft, used for technical ELINT collection, complete with bogus serial numbers applied to the nose and tail) are without doubt the most sophisticated air breathing intelligence gathering platforms in the western world. (Paul Crickmore Collection)

pinpointed immediately by triangulation. This method side-stepped the problems of emitters shutting down before the direction-finding process, conducted by Wild Weasel aircraft, could be completed. A similar system, known as the Advanced Location and Strike System (ALSS), had been installed together with datalinks on all seven remaining Air Force U-2Cs, back in 1972; however, it was plagued with problems and cancelled. The sophistication of PLSS brought with it similar difficulties and after a series of delays, it too was cancelled, in the late 1980s.

UK Operations

With ad hoc deployments to RAF Mildenhall of both the U-2R and SR-71 having been made during the late 1970s, Det 4 of the 9th SRW was established at the base in April 1979 with a single U-2R. Its mission was purely SigInt, however, as the year came to an end, 68-10338 was replaced by 68-10339. This latter aircraft was equipped with both Senior Ruby and Senior Spear, thereby combining both Elint and SigInt on a single airframe. Det 4 continued to fly the SigInt mission, codenamed Creak Spectre until February 1982, after which the role was taken on by TR-1As of the newly activated 17th Reconnaissance Wing, at RAF Alconbury. In March 1985, the 17th RW received three more TR-1As together with the ASARS-2 capability. A major milestone was achieved by Lt Col John Sander on 9 July 1985, when he flew the first operational ASARS-2 sortie, marking a new beginning in battlefield reconnaissance. The wing was eventually assigned twelve TR-1As before being deactivated in June 1991.

Desert Shield and Desert Storm

Just fifteen days after Iraq invaded Kuwait, two U-2s arrived at King Fahad Royal Saudi Air Base (RSAB). One aircraft, 80-1070, was equipped with Senior Span - a system for uplinking data from the SigInt collection systems to satellites, which then relayed the data across the globe. The other aircraft was equipped with SYERS -

Above and below The dorsal mounted pod houses a small dish antenna, enabling data to be transmitted to virtually any spot on earth, thanks to satellite relay. During the recent Balkan Wars, this development, known as Senior Span, integrated with Senior Glass (a combination of Senior Spear and Senior Ruby) enabled effective use to be made of all communications intelligence to a hitherto unattainable level. (Lockheed Martin)

the Senior Year Electro-optical Relay System. This system, developed by Itek, utilises a long focal length camera of 110 inches, with cassegrain or folding optics technology, to focus an image on a 10,240 element, Charged Couple Device (CCD). This digitised image, like ASARS, is then downloaded, in near-real time, to a ground station. On 19 August, both aircraft conducted their first operational missions near the Kuwait border. Four days later, two TR-1s arrived at King Fahad RSAB, from RAF Alconbury and on 29 August the first ASARS mission was flown. The new operating location at King Fahad was initially known as Location CH (Camel Hump), this was later redesignated 1704th Reconnaissance Squadron (Provisional) and was a component part of the 1700th Strategic Wing (Provisional). Ground stations for SYERS - codenamed Senior Blade, and for ASARS - known as TADMS - TR-1 ASARS Data Manipulation System, were located in a compound of the US Training Mission at Riyadh, where they were joined by stations to support RC-135 Rivet Joint Elint aircraft and J-STARS. A fifth U-2R (another SYERS equipped aircraft) arrived on 11 October, having been despatched from Osan AFB, South Korea.

From mid September, Iraq began launching MiG-25s in response to the U-2 border flights and henceforth they were provided with an F-15 MiG-Cap. The high level of systems integration derived from SYERS and ASARS ensured that within 10 minutes of a target being imaged by either system, its co-ordinate were available to the Theatre Air Control Centre. Indeed the system worked so well that when coalition attacks began, the nine U-2s (which soon became twelve) were virtually high altitude Forward Air Control (FAC) platforms detecting the positions of SA-2, SA-3 and AAA sites as well as 'Scud' missiles.

When the ground war began on 24 February, a TR-1 provided an hour-by-hour image 'commentary' of precise Iraqi front-line armour and troop movements, thereby contributing directly to the speed of the coalition advance. In all, the 1704th RS flew 260 missions, totalling over 2,000 hours. It was calculated that they had provided 50 per cent of all imagery intelligence and a staggering 90 per cent of the Army's targeting requirement.

Further Developments

In 1988, Hughes was granted a development contract to add a Moving Target Indicator (MTI) capability to ASARS. However, the actions of Saddam Hussein interrupted operational tests of the system, by the 17 RW.

After the Gulf War, tests were successfully completed in October 1991 and the ASARS MTI became operational four years later. Now the system is capable of locating moving targets in search or spot modes.

After much Air Force deliberation, it was decided to upgrade the U-2 fleet with the General Electric F101-GE-F29 turbofan engine. Of similar thrust to the J75, the newer engine promised to be much cheaper to maintain and was significantly lighter, with a much improved fuel consumption rate, thus restoring valuable performance lost through the expansion of the sensor package. It was first flown by Ken Weir in 80-1090 on 23 May 1989 and on 28 October 1994, a delivery ceremony was held at Palmdale, when the first three conversions were handed back to the Air Force, the engine having been redesignated in the meantime the F118.

Despite President Bush's optimistic remarks about the establishment of a new world order, following the collapse of communism in the Soviet Union, continued political instability in various parts of the world has ensured that the capabilities of the U-2 reconnaissance system are as much in demand today as they were back in 1956.

Below In all, 25 TR-1As, two TR-1Bs and two ER-2s were built using 'White World' money, at the Lockheed Martin Skunk Works plant at Palmdale - in addition, seven U-2Rs and a dual-control U-2R (T) were built 'in the black'. (Lockheed Martin)

The SR-71

Mindful of the subsonic vulnerability of the U-2 to developing Soviet SAM systems, the Agency's Richard Bissell contacted Kelly Johnson in the Autumn of 1957, and asked if the Lockheed Skunk Works team would conduct an operational analysis into the relationship of an aircraft's interceptibility, as a function of its speed, altitude and radar cross section (RCS). As Kelly was already immersed in related studies, he agreed to accept the project; the results of which concluded that flight at supersonic speed and extreme altitude, coupled with the use of radar absorbent materials (RAM) and radar attenuating design, greatly reduced, but not negated, the chances of radar detection and a successful interception. Encouraged by these results, it was agreed that further exploratory work should be conducted. During the closing months of 1957, the Agency invited Lockheed Aircraft Corporation and

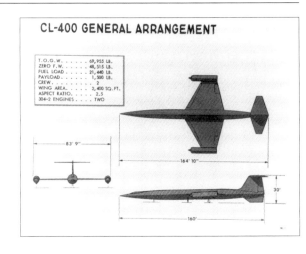

Above right With studies conducted by Pratt & Whitney and the Skunk Works at an advanced stage, Kelly Johnson proposed a liquid hydrogen propelled U-2 follow-on design to Lt Gen Donald Putt, during a Pentagon meeting in early January 1956. This Special Access Required programme, codenamed 'Suntan' developed the original CL-325 design into the CL-400. On paper, capable of Mach 2.5 at 100,000ft it was finally cancelled in February 1959, due primarily to lack of design stretch and logistical problems concerning the positioning of its highly volatile fuel. However the proposal led directly to a series of hydrocarbon designs that would take aerospace into a new era. (Lockheed Martin)

Opposite top A shot taken early in the A-12 test programme depicts a bare titanium aircraft landing at Area 51.

Above A-12 933 is seen outside one of the specially constructed 'barns'. (CIA)

Right Seven single seat A-12s, one two-seat trainer and two YF-12As are seen lined up in their black and titanium paint scheme. The black paint hides wedges of radar absorbent material (RAM), that frame the aircraft's planform. (CIA)

the Convair Division of General Dynamics to field to them non-funded, non-contracted design submissions for a reconnaissance gathering vehicle, which adhered to the aforementioned performance criteria. Both companies accepted the challenge and were assured that funding would be forthcoming at the appropriate time. For the next twelve months, the Agency received designs that were both developed and refined, all at no expense!

It was however, readily apparent to Bissell that the cost of developing such an advanced aircraft would be both high-risk and extremely expensive; government funding would be a prerequisite and to obtain this, various high-ranking government officials would have to be cleared into the programme and given concis, authoritative presentations on advances as they occurred. He therefore assembled a highly talented panel of six specialists under the chair of Dr Edwin Land. Between 1957 and 1959 the panel met on some six occasions, usually in Land's Cambridge, Massachusetts office. Kelly and General Dynamics' Vincent Dolson were at times in attendance, as were the Assistant Secretaries of the Air Force, Navy and

Above When deployed to Kadena under operation Blackshield, A-12s sported an overall black scheme, carrying no national insignia and bogus serials. (CIA)

Below Agency pilot Ken Collins ejected safely from '926 on 24 May 1963. He is seen here wearing a David Clark S-901 full pressure suit. (CIA)

other select technical advisors. Code-named project Gusto by the Agency, Lockheed's first submission, Archangel, proposed a Mach 3 cruise aircraft with a range of 4,000 nautical miles at altitudes of between 90-95,000 ft. This, together with his Gusto Model G2A submission, was well received by the Programme Office, as Kelly noted later. Convair on the other hand prepared the Super Hustler; Mach-4 capable, ramjet-powered when launched from a B-58 and turbojet assisted for landing. As designs were refined and re-submitted, the Lockheed offerings became shortened to A, followed by an index number, these ran from A-3 to A-12. The design and designations from Convair also evolved and on 20th August 1959, final submissions from both companies were made to a joint DoD/Air Force/CIA selection panel. Though strikingly

different, the proposed performance of each aircraft was on a par.

On 28 August 1959, Kelly was told by the director of the programme that Lockheed's Skunk Works had won the competition to build the U-2 follow-on. The next day they were given the official go-ahead, with initial funding of $4.5 million approved to cover the period 1 September to 1 January 1960. Project Gusto was now at an end and a new code name, Oxcart, was assigned. On 3 September, the Agency authorised Lockheed to proceed with anti-radar studies, aerodynamic, structural tests and engineering designs.

The small engineering team, under the supervision of Ed Martin, consisted of Dan Zuck in charge of cockpit design, Dave Robertson fuel system requirements, Henry Combs and Dick Bochme structures, Dick Fuller, Burt McMaster and Kelly's protege Ben Rich.

The ambitious performance sought in the new aircraft can't be overstated: the best front-line fighter aircraft of the day were the early century-series jets, like the F-100 Super Sabre and F-101 Voodoo. In a single bound, the A-12 would operate at sustained speeds and altitudes treble and double respectively, of such contemporary fighters' limits. The technical challenge facing the Skunk Works team was vast and the contracted time scale in which to achieve it was incredibly tight. Kelly would later remark that virtually everything on the aircraft had to be invented from scratch. Operating above 80,000 feet the ambient air temperature was minus 56 degrees Centigrade and the atmospheric air pressure just 0.4 pounds per square inch. But cruising at a speed of a mile every two seconds, airframe temperatures would vary from 245 to 565 degrees Centigrade.

Sustained operation in such an extreme temperature environment, meant lavish use of advanced titanium alloys, which account for 85 per cent of the aircraft's structural weight, the remaining 15 per cent was comprised of composite materials. The decision to use such materials was based upon titanium's ability to withstand high operating temperatures. It weighs half as much as stainless steel but has the same tensile strength; in addition, conventional construction was possible using fewer parts - high strength composites weren't available in the early sixties. The particular titanium used was B-120VCA, which can be hardened to strengths of up to 200 Ksi. Initially the ageing process required 70 hours to achieve maximum strength but, with careful processing techniques, this was reduced to 40 hours. A rigorous (and expensive) quality control programme was set up, wherein

Top left Aircraft '932 was lost during a functional check flight (FCF) just prior to being redeployed back to the United States on 5 June 1968; its pilot, Jack Weeks, was killed in the incident. (CIA)

Top right The classified unit designation of the CIA, A-12 desert dwellers, was the 1129th Special Activities Squadron, 'The Road Runners'. (Paul Crickmore Collection)

Above When the A-12 programme was cancelled, the remaining aircraft were flown from Area 51 to Palmdale and placed in storage. (Lockheed Martin)

for every batch of ten or more parts processed, three samples were heat treated to the same level as those in the batch. One was then strength-tested to destruction, another tested for formability and the third held in reserve should processing be required. With more than 13 million titanium parts manufactured, data is available on all but a few. Using this advanced material involved a steep learning curve and it wasn't long before problems arose. Titanium is not compatible with chlorine, fluorine or cadmium. A line for example, drawn on sheet titanium with a Pentel pen, will eat a hole through it in about 12 hours - all Pentel pens were recalled from the shop floor. Early spot welded panels produced during the summer had a habit of failing, while those built in the winter lasted indefinitely. Diligent detective work discovered that to

prevent the formation of algae in the summer, the Burbank water supply was heavily chlorinated. Subsequently, the Skunk Works washed all titanium parts in distilled water. As thermodynamic tests got underway bolt heads began dropping from installations; this, it was discovered, was caused by tiny cadmium deposits, left after cadium-plated spanners had been used to apply torque. As the bolts were heated in excess of 320 degrees Centigrade, their heads simply dropped off. Remedy: all cadium-plated tools were removed from tool boxes.

Another test undertaken studied thermal effects on large titanium wing panels. An element 4ft x 6ft (1.2 x 1.8m) was heated to the computed heat flux expected in flight and resulted in the sample warping into a totally unacceptable shape. This problem was resolved by manufacturing chordwise corrugations into the outer skins. At the design heat rate, the corrugations merely deepened by a few thousandths of an inch and on cooling returned to the basic shape. Kelly recalled he was accused of "trying to make a 1932 Ford Trimotor go Mach 3", but added that "the concept worked fine". To prevent this titanium outer skin from tearing when secured to heavier substructures, the Skunk Works developed stand-off clips, this ensured structural continuity while creating a heat shield between adjacent components.

Chosen powerplant would be the Pratt & Whitney JT11D-20 engine (designated J58 by the US military). This high bypass ratio afterburning engine was the result of two earlier, ill-fated programmes: Project Suntan (see p34, caption) together with Pratt & Whitney's JT9 single-spool high pressure ratio turbojet rated at 26,000lbs in afterburner and developed for a US Navy attack aircraft, which was also axed. Nevertheless, the engine had already completed 700 hours of full-scale engine testing and results were very encouraging. As testing continued however, it became apparent that due to the incredibly hostile thermal conditions of sustained Mach 3.2 flight, only the basic airflow size (400 lbs per second of airflow) and the compressor and turbine aerodynamics of the original Navy J58 P2 engine could be retained (even these were later modified). The stretched design criteria, associated with high Mach number and its related large air-flow turn-down ratio, led to the development of a variable cycle, later known as a bleed-bypass engine; a

Above Pictured at Area 51 with another A-12 just visible behind the gantry, M-21, Article 134, serial 60-6940, is seen with a D-21 mounted on its dorsal pylon. (Lockheed Martin)

Above right To aid 'Mother/Daughter' separation, a cylinder of compressed air was carried in the pylon. (Lockheed Martin)

Below This shot, believed to be that of the ill-fated M-21, serial 60-6941, shows the aircraft in a later overall black scheme. (Lockheed Martin)

concept conceived by Pratt & Whitney's Robert Abernathy. This eliminated many airflow problems through the engine, by bleeding air from the fourth stage of the nine-stage, single-spool axial-flow compressor. This excess air was passed through six low-compression-ratio bypass ducts and re-introduced into the turbine exhaust, near the front of the afterburner, at the same static pressure as the main flow. This reduced exhaust gas temperature (EGT) and produced almost as much thrust per pound of air as the main flow, which had passed through the rear compressor, the burner section and the turbine. Scheduling of the bypass bleed was achieved by the main fuel control as a function of compressor inlet temperature (CIT) and engine rpm. Bleed air injection occurred at a CIT of between 85 and 115 degrees Centigrade (approximately Mach 1.9). To further minimise stalling the front stages of the rotor blades at low engine speeds, moveable inlet guide vanes (IGVs) were incorporated to help guide airflow to the compressor. These changed from an axial, to a cambered position, in response to the main fuel control, which regulated most engine functions. In the 'axial' position, additional thrust was provided for take off and acceleration to intermediate supersonic speeds, the IGVs then moved to the 'cambered' position, when the CIT reached 85 to 115 degrees Centigrade. Should IGV 'lock-in' fail to occur upon reaching a CIT of 150 degrees Centigrade, the mission was aborted.

When operating at cruising speeds, the turbine inlet

three Dewar flasks situated in the front nose gear well was also used to provide a positive 'head' of gaseous nitrogen in the fuel tanks. This prevented the depleted tanks from crushing as the aircraft descended into the denser atmosphere, to land or refuel. In addition, the inert gas reduced the risk of inadvertent vapour ignition.

Oxcart received a shot in the arm on 30 January 1960, when the Agency gave Lockheed ADP the go-ahead to manufacture and test a dozen A-12s, including one two-seat conversion trainer. With Lockheed's' chief test pilot, Louis W Schalk now on board, work on refining the aircraft's design continued in parallel with additional construction work at Area 51. A new water well was drilled and new recreation facilities were provided for the construction workers, who were billeted in trailer houses. A new 8,500 ft runway was constructed and 18 miles of off-base highway were resurfaced to allow half a million gallons of PF-1 fuel to be trucked in every month. Three US Navy hangars together with Navy housing units were transported to the site in readiness for the arrival of the A-12 prototype, expected in May 1961. However, difficulties in procuring and working with titanium, together with problems experienced by Pratt & Whitney, soon began to compound and the anticipated first flight date slipped. Even when the completion date was put back to Christmas and the initial test flight postponed to late February 1962, the first J58s would still not be ready. Eventually Kelly decided that J75 engines would be used in the interim to propel the A-12 to a 'half-way house' of 50,000 ft and Mach 1.6, this action took at least some of the pressure off the test team.

The flight crew selection process evolved by the

temperature (TIT) reached over 1100 degrees Centigrade; this necessitated the development of a unique fuel, developed jointly by Pratt & Whitney, Ashland Shell and Monsanto, known originally as PF-1 and latterly as JP-7. Having a much higher ignition temperature than JP-4, standard electrical ignition systems were useless. Instead a chemical ignition system (CIS), was developed, using a highly volatile pyrophoric fluid known as tri-ethyl borane (TEB). Extremely flash sensitive when oxidised, a small TEB tank was carried on the aircraft to allow engine afterburner start-up both on the ground and when aloft; the tank was pressurised using gaseous nitrogen, to ensure the system remained inert. Liquid nitrogen carried in

Pentagon's Special Activities Office representative (Col Houser Wilson) and the Agency's USAF liaison officer (Brig Gen Jack Ledford, later succeeded by Brig Paul Bacalis), got under way in 1961. On completion of the final screening, the first pilots were William Skliar, Kenneth Collins, Walter Ray, Alonzo Walter, Mele Vojvodich, Jack Weeks, Jack Layton, Dennis Sullivan, David Young, Francis Murray and Russ Scott (only six of the above were destined to fly operational missions). These elite pilots then began taking trips to the David Clark Company in Worcester, Massachusetts, to be outfitted with their own personal S-901 full pressure suits –

Bbove When Tagboard was cancelled, two B-52Hs of the 4200th Test Wing, at Beale AFB, continued working with the D-21s, which required rocket boosters to propel them to their cruise speed and altitude. (Lockheed Martin)

Below The North American F-108 Rapier was to have been an Improved Manned Interceptor (IMI) capable of Mach 3. It was cancelled due to escalating costs. (Rockwell International)

just like those worn by the Mercury and Gemini astronauts. In late 1961, Col Robert Holbury was appointed Base Commander of Area 51, his Director of Flight Operations would be Col Doug Nelson. In the spring of 1962 eight F-101 Voodoos, to be used as companion trainers and to pace-chase, two T-33s for pilot proficiency and a C-130, for cargo transportation, arrived at the remote base. A large 'restricted airspace zone' was enforced by the Federal Aviation Agency (FAA), to enhance security around 'the Area' and security notices were brought to the attention of North American Air Defence (NORAD) and FAA radar controllers, to ensure that fast-moving targets seen on their screens weren't discussed. Planned air refuelling operations of Oxcart aircraft would be conducted by the 903rd Air Refuelling Squadron, located at Beale AFB, and equipped with KC-135Q tankers which possessed separate 'clean' tankage and plumbing to isolate the A-12s' fuel from the tankers' JP4, and special ARC-50 distance-ranging radios for use in precision, long distance, high-speed join ups.

With the first A-12 now at last ready for final assembly, the entire fuselage, minus wings, was created, covered with canvas and loaded on a special $100,000 trailer. At 2.30am on 26 February 1962, the slow moving convoy left Burbank and arrived safely at Area 51 at 1.00pm, two days later. By 24 April, engine test runs together with low- and medium-speed taxi tests had been successfully completed. It was now time for Lou Schalk to take to the aircraft on a high-speed taxi run that would culminate in a momentary lift off and landing roll-out onto the dry salt lake-bed. For this first 'hop' the stability augmentation system (SAS) was left uncoupled; it would be properly tested in flight. As A-12 article number 121 accelerated down the runway, Lou recalled:-
"I had a very light load of fuel so it sort of accelerated

really fast … I was probably three or four per cent behind the aft limit centre of gravity when I lifted off the airplane, so it was unstable … Immediately after lift-off, I really didn't think I was going to be able to put the airplane back on the ground safely because of lateral, directional and longitudinal oscillations. The airplane was very difficult to handle but I finally caught up with everything that was happening, got control back enough to set it back down, and chop engine power. Touchdown was on the lake bed instead of the runway, creating a tremendous cloud of dust into which I disappeared entirely. The tower controllers were calling me to find

Below Developed for the F-108, the Hughes ASG-18 radar intercept system, together with its GAR-9 missile, remained under development and both were flight tested in this specially modified B-58, nicknamed 'Snoopy 1', due to its extended nose profile. Note camera pods under outboard engines to record missile separations. (Paul Crickmore Collection)

Bottom Kelly, up at Area 51, stands next to the third and final YF-12A interceptor, Article 1003, serial 60-6936. (Lockheed Martin)

out what was happening and I was answering, but the UHF antenna was located on the underside of the airplane (for best transmission in flight) and no one could hear me. Finally, when I slowed down and started my turn on the lake bed and re-emerged from the dust cloud, everyone breathed a sigh of relief."

Two days later Lou took the Oxcart on a full flight. A faultless 07:05am take off was followed shortly thereafter by all the left wing fillets being shed. Constructed from RAM, luckily these elements were non-structural and Lou recovered the aircraft back to Area 51 without further incident.

On 30 April - nearly a year behind schedule - Lou took the A-12 on its 'official' first flight. With appropriate government representatives on hand the 59-minute flight took the aircraft to a top speed and altitude of 340kts and 30,000ft. On 4 May, the aircraft went supersonic for the first time, reaching Mach 1.1. Kelly began to feel confident that the flight test programme would now progress rapidly, even recovering some time lost during the protracted manufacturing process. Another Lockheed test pilot, Bill Park joined the Skunk Works team to share the burden with Lou. On 26 June, the second A-12 arrived at Area 51 and was immediately assigned to a three-month static RCS test programme. The third and fourth aircraft arrived during October and November, the latter was a two-seat A-12 trainer, nicknamed 'the Goose' by its crews. The aircraft was powered throughout its life by two J75s. On 5 October, another milestone was achieved when the A-12 flew for the first time with a J58, (a J75 was retained in the right nacelle until 15 January 1963, when the first fully J58-powered flight took place).

When Randy Anderson's U-2 was shot down by an SA-2 over Cuba on 27 October 1962, the U-2's vulnerability was once again demonstrated in spectacular fashion. The significance of the incident was certainly not lost on

Above YF-12 A prototype, Article 1001, serial 60-6934, makes a low, fast pass for the cameras. Note the extended ventral fin together with the fins under its engine nacelles to improve longitudinal stability, together with the under-side camera pods to record missile separation and the IR sensor in the forward chine below the cockpit. (Lockheed Martin)

Below Boeing JQB-47E-45BO, serial 53-4256, was one of a number of remotely piloted B-47 drones used to evaluate missile and radar performance. It was operated by the 3214th drone maintenance Squadron, at Eglin AFB, during the YF-12 trials off Florida. Note stencilling. (Paul Crickmore Collection)

Right When the YF-12 programme was cancelled Col J Sullivan and Col R Uppstrom ferried the aircraft to Wright-Patterson AFB where it is now on permanent display at the Air Force Museum as the sole surviving example. (Lockheed Martin)

intelligence communities involved in Oxcart and the successful prosecution of that programme now became a matter of highest national priority.

A third Lockheed test pilot, Jim Eastham, was recruited into Oxcart, but still the programme was beset with problems, most of which were focused around the engines and Air Inlet Control System (AICS). The AICS regulated massive internal air flow throughout the aircraft's vast flight envelope, controlling and supplying air to the engines at the correct velocity and pressure. This was achieved using a combination of bypass doors and translating centre-body spike position. At ground idle, taxiing and take-off, the spikes were positioned in the full-forward position, allowing air to flow unimpeded to the engine's compressor face. In addition, supplementary flow was provided through the spike exit-louvres and from six forward bypass exit-louvres. Early tests revealed that the engine required an even greater supply of air when operating at low power settings. This deficiency was overcome by installing additional bypass doors just forward of the compressor face. The size of these variable-area 'inlet ports' was regulated by an external slotted-band and could draw air through two sets of doors. The task of opening or closing these doors was manually controlled by the pilot initially, but this was accomplished much later automatically, when a Digital Automatic Flight Inlet Control System (DAFICS) computer was developed. Together, the forward bypass doors and the centre-body spikes were used to control the position of the normal shockwave just aft of the inlet throat. To avoid the loss of inlet efficiency, caused by an improperly positioned shockwave, the wave was captured and held inside the converging-diverging nozzle slightly behind the narrowest part of the 'throat', allowing the maximum pressure rise across the normal shock. Once airborne with landing gear retracted, the forward bypass doors closed automatically. At Mach 1.4 the doors began to modulate automatically to obtain a programmed pressure ratio between 'dynamic' pressure at the inlet cowl on one side of the 'throat' and 'static' duct pressure on the other side. At 30,000ft and Mach 1.6, the inlet spike unlocked and commenced its rearward translation, completing its full aft movement of 26 inches at designated speed Mach 3.2 (the inlet's most efficient speed). Spike scheduling was determined as a function of Mach number, with a bias for abnormal angle of attack, angle of side slip, or rate of vertical acceleration. The rearward translation of the spike gradually repositioned the oblique shock wave, which extended back from the spike tip, and the normal shockwave, standing at right angles to the air flow, and increased the inlet contraction ratio (the ratio between the inlet area and the 'throat' area). At Mach 3.2, with the spike fully aft, the

'capture-airstream-tube-area' had increased 112 per cent (from 8.7sq ft to 18.5 sq ft), while the 'throat' restriction had decreased to 46 per cent of its former size (from 7.7 sq ft to 4.16 sq ft).

A peripheral 'shock trap' bleed slot (positioned around the inside surface of the duct, just forward of the 'throat' and set at precisely two boundary layer displacement thickness) 'shaved' off seven per cent of the inlet airflow and stabilised the terminal (normal) shock. This was then rammed across the bypass plenum, through 32 shock trap tubes, spaced at regular intervals around the circumference of the shock trap. As the compressed air travelled through the secondary passage, it firmly closed the suck-in doors while cooling the exterior of the engine casing before exhausting through the ejector nozzle. Boundary layer air was also removed from the surface of the centre-body spike at the point if its maximum diameter. This potentially turbulent air was then ducted through the spikes hollow supporting struts and dumped overboard, through nacelle exit louvres. The bypass system was thus able to match widely varying volumes of air entering the inlet system, with an equal volume of air leaving the ejector nozzle throughout the entire speed range of the aircraft.

The aft bypass doors were opened at mid Mach to minimise the aerodynamic drag which resulted from dumping air overboard through the forward bypass doors. The inlet system created internal pressures which reached 18lbs per square inch when operating at Mach 3.2 and 80,000ft, where the ambient air pressure was only 0.4lbs per square inch. This extremely large pressure differential generated

Above Between 11 December 1969 and 31 October 1979, NASA and the US Air Force embarked upon a joint high altitude test programme which required the use of two YF-12s and an SR-71. YF-12 60-6936 however was lost on 24 June 1971; both Lt Col 'Jack' Layton and Systems Operator Maj Bill Curtis ejected safely. SR-71A, Article 2002, serial 64-17951 was redesignated YF-12C for political reasons and given the serial number 60-6937. (NASA)

Below The NASA flight test team were (left to right) Ray Young, Fitzhugh Fulton, Donald Mallick and Victor Horton. (NASA)

Above and above right The redesigned forward forebody of the YF-12 compared to an SR-71 is immediately apparent. (Lockheed Martin)

Right This Skunk Works document dated 6 April 1967, shows what the Air Force could have had - a Mach 3.2 reconnaissance aircraft, SR-71- a bomber, B-71- and interceptor, F-12. (Paul Crickmore Collection)

a pressure gradient, which in turn created a forward thrust vector, resulting in the forward inlet producing 54 per cent of the total thrust. A further 29 per cent was produced by the ejector, while the J58 engine contributed only 17 per cent of the total thrust at high Mach.

Inlet airflow disturbances resulted if the delicate balance of airflow conditions that maintained the shock-wave in its normal position were upset. Such disturbances were called 'unstarts'. These disruptions occurred when the normally-placed supersonic shockwave was 'belched' forward from a balanced position in the inlet throat, causing an instant drop in inlet pressure and thrust. With the engines mounted at mid-semi-span, the shockwave departure manifested itself in a vicious yaw toward the 'unstarted' inlet. Sometimes these were so violent that crew members' helmets would be knocked hard against the canopy framing. To break a sustained unstart and recapture the disturbed inlet shock wave, the pilot would have to open the bypass doors on the unstarted inlet and return them to the smooth-flowing, but less efficient position that they had occupied prior to the disturbance.

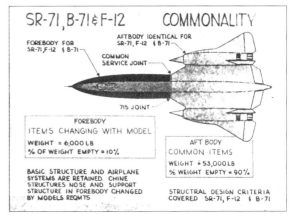

SR-71, B-71 & F-12   COMMONALITY

FOREBODY FOR
SR-71, F-12 & B-71

AFTBODY IDENTICAL FOR
SR-71, F-12 & B-71

COMMON
SERVICE JOINT

715 JOINT

FOREBODY
ITEMS CHANGING WITH MODEL
WEIGHT = 6,000 LB
% OF WEIGHT EMPTY = 10%

AFT BODY
COMMON ITEMS
WEIGHT ≈ 53,000 LB
% WEIGHT EMPTY = 90%

BASIC STRUCTURE AND AIRPLANE
SYSTEMS ARE RETAINED. CHINE
STRUCTURES NOSE AND SUPPORT
STRUCTURE IN FOREBODY CHANGED
BY MODELS REQMTS

STRUCTRAL DESIGN CRITERIA
COVERED SR-71, F-12 & B-71

Early A-12 test flights involved increasing the aircraft's speed by increments of one tenth of a Mach number and manually selecting the next spike position. If the inlet dynamics worked well, the aircraft was decelerated and recovered back to 'the Area'; there the dynamics would be further analysed and incorporated. More often however there would be a mismatch between spike position and inlet duct requirements and a vicious unstart would result. In all, it took 66 flights to push the speed envelope out from Mach 2.0 to Mach 3.2 and it wasn't until pneumatic pressure gauges, installed on the inlet systems to sense pressure variations of as little as one-quarter of a pound per square inch, were replaced by an electrically controlled system from aircraft number nine (60-6932) onwards, that the incidence of unstarts plummetted.

The YF-12

During December 1960, a separate project group working independently of the A-12 team, under Rus Daniell, was organised in the Skunk Works. From joint 715, (a point perpendicular to where the inboard wing leading edge meets the fuselage chine), the entire forward fuselage forebody of an A-12 was modified to create a Mach 3.2 interceptor. Originally designated AF-12, its 1,380lb Hughes AN/ASG-18 pulse Doppler radar and 818 lbs GAR-9 missile, had been intended for the North American F-108 Rapier, however following cancellation on 23 September 1959, DoD officials decided that development of this outstanding system should continue on a 'stand alone' basis. Therefore Hughes continued R&D

Above Bob Gilliland completes a fly by in '950 on its maiden flight over runway 25 at Palmdale. He is being chased by Jim Eastham in F-104 60790. (Lockheed Martin)

Below Lockheed test pilot Bill Weaver survived a Mach 3.1 break-up accident at an altitude of 81,000ft, in SR-71A, 64-17952, on 25 January 1966. Tragically, his flight test engineer, Jim Zwayer was killed. (Lockheed Martin)

Below right SR-71A 64-17953 crashed on 18 December 1969 after an inflight explosion. Lt Col Joe Rogers and RSO Lt Col Garry Heidlebaugh ejected safely. (Lockheed Martin)

Below, right and below right Lt Col Bill Skliar (pictured) and his RSO, Maj Noel Warner, had a lucky escape at Edwards on 11 April 1969, when a wheel disintegrated on rotation and set 80,000 lbs of JP-7 ablaze. Luckily both men managed to escape uninjured. SR-71A, 64-17954 however, was written off. (Paul Crickmore Collection)

work with both systems utilising a specially modified Convair B-58A Hustler.

On 31 May 1960, the Air Force conducted a mock-up review of the AF-12 and were duly impressed. By June, AF-12 wind turned tests revealed directional stability problems resulting from the heavily revised nose profile and cockpit configuration. As a result a large folding fin was mounted under the aft fuselage, as were two shorter fixed fins beneath each nacelle. A bomber version of the A-12, designated the RB-12, also reached the mock-up stage, but this would prove to be still-born, as it represented too much of a threat to the highly political North American XB-70A Valkyrie. On 7 August 1963, several weeks after being moved to Area 51, Jim Eastham climbed aboard the interceptor prototype and took aircraft 60-6934 (the seventh A-12), for its first flight; a flight he would later modestly describe as a 'typical production test flight'.

On 24 May 1963, the program received a temporary set back when Agency pilot Ken Collins was forced to eject from A-12 60-6926, during a subsonic test flight. The crash occurred 14 miles south of Wendover, Utah; a press cover story referred to the aircraft as being a Republic F-105 Thunderchief, thus preserving security. An accident investigation established the cause of the incident to be a pilot-static system failure due to icing.

As 1963 drew to a close, nine A-12s at Groom Lake had notched up a total of 573 flights totalling 765 hours. A year later, eleven A-12s had logged over 1,214 flights amounting to 1,669 hours - only 6 hours 23 minutes however was at Mach 3 and only 33 minutes at design

speed, Mach 3.2. As Oxcart grew in size and cost, concern was expressed within both the Agency and Air Force as to how much longer the program could be kept a secret. It was also noted that technological data accumulated during the project would be of immense value in conjunction with 'white world' feasibility studies into supersonic passenger transport. In November 1963, President Johnson was briefed on the programme, after which he directed that a formal announcement be prepared for release early in the new year. Kelly Johnson noted in his diary "Plans going forward for surfacing of the AF-12 program. I worked on the draft to be used by President Johnson and proposed the terminology 'A-11' as it was the non-anti-radar version." On Saturday 29 February 1964, a few hours prior to the President announcing the existence of part of the programme, two AF-12s, 60-6934 and 60-6935 were flown from Area 51 to Edwards AFB, by Lou Schalk and Bob Gilliland, thereby diverting attention away from Area 51 and the 'black world' A-12 programme. At Edwards a 'buzz' had gone out to a few senior staff that something special might be happening on the first morning of their weekend off. In consequence, a few dozen people witnessed the arrival of the extremely sleek interceptor, the like of which no one outside the programme had seen - except for a few desert dwellers and the occasional incredulous sighting by airline crews. Lou Schalk recalls taxying to their assigned hangar as eyes bulged and heads nodded in utter disbelief. Unfortunately, the arrival lost a touch of elegance when, to aid push-back into the hangar, they turned the aircraft through 180 degrees. Lou recalls " This turnaround sent hot engine exhaust gases flooding into the hangar which caused the overhead fire extinguishers valves to open. These valves were big - like the flood valves on hangar decks of aircraft carriers - and the desert hadn't seen so much water since Noah's embarkation!"

Above The rear fuselage section, aft of joint 715, is moved on to the next jig. (Lockheed Martin)

Below Temperatures excounted whilst at cruise speed and altitude dictated the use of titanium. (Lockheed Martin)

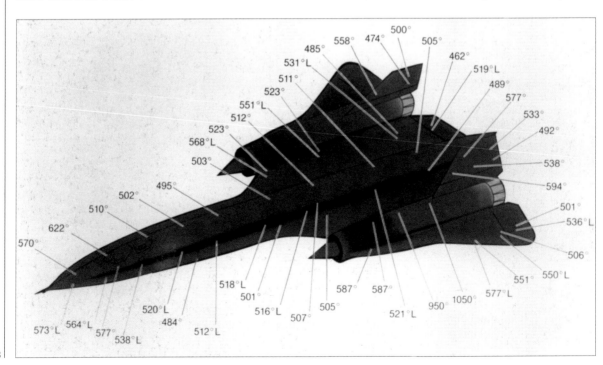

Now an Air Force program, the aircraft's designation was changed to YF-12A to suit their system. The third YF-12A, 60-6936, soon joined the other two at Edwards and Jim Eastham continued the envelope expansion programme. On 16 April 1964, the first airborne AIM-47 missile separation test was conducted. Unfortunately, as onboard cameras showed, the weapon's nose-down pitch was inadequate: had the rocket motor ignition also been fired, the missile would probably have ended up in the front cockpit! Back at 'the Ranch', on 9 July 1964, Bill Park experienced a complete lock-up of his flight controls in aircraft 60-6939 as he descended for landing following a high Mach flight. Despite trying to save the brand-new aircraft from rolling under while turning on to final approach, he couldn't stop the bank angle from increasing and was forced to eject. Punching out at 200kts in a 34 degree bank, no more than 200 ft above the ground, Park was extremely lucky to survive unscathed.

A milestone in the programme was reached on 27 January 1965, when an A-12 flew a 2,580 mile sortie in one hour forty minutes, with three-quarters of the flight time spent at Mach 3.1. On 18 March, YF-12A '935 successfully engaged a Q-2C target drone at 40,000ft, whilst the interceptor flew at Mach 2.2 and 65,000ft. Then on 1 May 1965 (five years to the day that Gary Powers was shot down in his U-2), YF-12A 60-6936 siezed back from the Soviet Union six world speed and altitude records. Fourteen days later, the Skunk Works

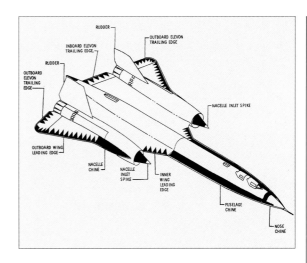

Above To reduce the SR-71's radar signature, radar absorbent material (RAM) is used. (Lockheed Martin)

Below An ingenious stand-off clip, developed by Skunk Works engineers, overcame the problem of attaching thin titanium sheets to bulkier structural components, without the former tearing due to expansion rates differentials. (Lockheed Martin)

Above The SR-71 is powered by two Pratt & Whitney JT11D-20 engines, designated J58 by the military. (Paul Crickmore)

Below and bottom To regulate the amount of air required by the propulsion system throughout its vast operating envelope, the centrebody spike translates back and forth. (Paul Crikcmore)

received a contract for $500,000 for the production version of the interceptor, designated F-12B. However, production go-ahead was not given with the engineering contract. Nonetheless, considerable optimism was generated. A further half-million dollars was granted on 10 November to keep basic F-12B design work alive. Similarly, Hughes received $4.5 million to continue development of the AN/ASG-18 radar and fire control system.

On 29 March 1966, Kelly had a long meeting with Col Ben Bellis, System Project Officer (SPO) at Hughes Aircraft Company and various members of the F-12 test force, during which he was asked to take on the task of integrating the weapons systems; this he agreed to do and fire control tests were continued. However, Secretary of Defence McNamara opposed production of the aircraft. As a result, on three occasions over the intervening two years, he denied the Air Force access to $90 million worth of funds which had been appropriated by Congress to begin F-12B production. Following a Senate Armed Services Committee hearing into the future of continental air defence, it was decided, in the light of intelligence

available at the time, to downgrade Aerospace Defence Command, which rendered the F-12B unnecessary. On 5 January 1968, official notification was received from the Air Force to 'close down the F-12B'; the YF-12A programme was formally ended on 1 February 1968. It would be the Blackworld, A-12 Oxcart program that validated the concept of sustained high Mach flight, but there was still a way to go …

Agency A-12 Operations

By late 1965, all of the Agency pilots were Mach 3 qualified and the A-12 was ready for operational testing. Despite this, political sensitivities surrounding the Gary Powers shoot-down five years earlier ensured that the aircraft would never carry out missions over the USSR. Where then should this multi-million dollar national security asset be deployed? The initial answer was Cuba. By early 1964, Project Headquarters had already begun planning contingency overflights under a programme code-name 'Skylark'. On 5 August 1965, the Director of

the National Security Agency (NSA), Gen Marshall S Carter, directed that "Skylark achieve emergency operational readiness by 5 November"; this was indeed achieved, but there was never a deployment. Instead Cygnus, as Agency pilots referred to the A-12, would receive its baptism of fire in the skies over South East Asia. Moves to this end had begun on 22 March 1965 when, following a meeting with Brig Gen Jack Ledford (the CIA/USAF liaison officer), Secretary of Defence (Sec Def) Cyrus Vance, granted $3.7 million to provide support facilities at Kadena AB, Okinawa for a planned deployment of Cygnus aircraft under a project code-named Blackshield. On 3 June, secretary McNamara consulted the under Secretary of the Air Force about the build-up of SA-2s around Hanoi and the possibility of substituting the more vulnerable U-2s with A-12s to conduct recce flights over the North Vietnamese capital. He was informed that once adequate aircraft performance was validated, Blackshield could be cleared to go.

Four aircraft were selected for Blackshield operations, Kelly Johnson taking personal responsibility for ensuring

Left To allow engine access for maintenance, the entire outer wing section is hinged along the top nacelle. (Paul Crickmore)

Below At the heart of the SR-71's propulsion is a complex Air Inlet Control System (AICS), utilising a combination of bypass doors, territory doors, the centre spike and suck in doors, to regulate and balance total airflow in order to reach the aircraft's designated sustained cruise speed of Mach 3.2. (Paul Crickmore Collection)

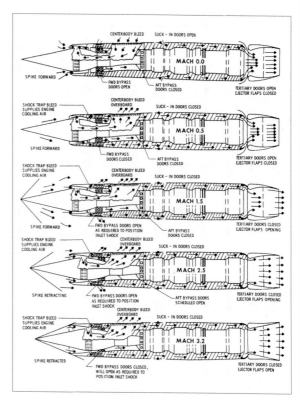

they were completely 'squawk-free'. On 20 November 1965 an A-12 completed a maximum endurance flight of six hours twenty minutes, during which it reached speeds above Mach 3.2 and altitudes approaching 90,000ft. On 2 December, the highly secretive '303 Committee' received the first of many proposals to deploy Oxcart to the Far East. However, the proposal, together with several subsequent submissions made throughout 1966, was rejected. On 5 January 1967, another tragedy hit the programme when A-12 60-6928 crashed some 70 miles short of Groom Dry Lake. Its pilot Walt Ray ejected but was killed when he was unable to gain seat separation.

In early May 1967, the National Security Council was briefed that North Vietnam was about to receive surface-to-surface ballistic missiles. Such a serious escalation of the conflict would certainly need to be substantiated with hard evidence, consequently President Johnson was briefed. Richard Helms of the CIA proposed that the 303 committee authorise deployment of Oxcart, on the basis of the A-12s having a superior camera to that used by U-2s or pilotless drones and being 'invulnerable to shoot-downs'. President Johnson approved the plan and in mid-May an airlift was begun to establish Blackshield at Kadena AB, on Okinawa, Japan.

At 0800 on 22 May 1967 Mele Vojvodich deployed A-12 60-6937 from Area 51 to Okinawa during a flight which lasted six hours, six minutes and included three air refuellings. Two days later Jack Layton joined Mele in 60-6930 and 60-6932 flown by Jack Weeks arrived on Okinawa on the 27th, having been forced to divert into Wake Island for a day, following INS and radio problems. The detachment was declared ready for operations on 29 May and following weather reconnaissance flights of the 30th, it was determined that conditions were ideal for

an A-12 camera run over North Vietnam. Project Headquarters in Washington placed Blackshield on alert for its first operational mission. Avionics specialists checked various systems and sensors, and at 1600hrs Mele Vojvodich and back-up pilot Jack Layton attended a mission alert briefing. At 2200hrs (12 hours before planned take-of time) a review of the weather confirmed

Above A wide variety of specialist support equipment was needed; shown here are liquid oxygen trailers. (Paul Crickmore)

Right The SR-71's cockpit certainly reflects its age - no multifunctional displays here! (Paul Crickmore)

Below The Reconnaissance Systems Officer's position is by comparison a little more user-friendly, as seen in this shot of the simulator at Edwards. (Paul Crickmore)

the mission was still on, so the pilots went to bed to ensure they got a full eight hours of crew rest.

They awoke on the morning of the 31st to torrential rain - a new phenomenon to desert-dwelling A-12s. However met conditions over 'the collection area' were good and at 0800 Kadena received a final 'go' from Washington. On cue, Mele engaged both afterburners and made the first instrument-guided take-off of an A-12. A few minutes later he burst through cloud and flew 60-6937 up to 25,000ft, topped-off the tanks from a KC-135, then accelerated and climbed to operational speed and altitude. With all systems up and running, he informed Kadena ('home-plate'), that the backup services of Jack Layton wouldn't be required. Mele penetrated hostile airspace at Mach 3.2 and 80,000ft over Haiphong, before overflying Hanoi and exiting North Vietnam near Dien Bien Phu. A second air refuelling took place over Thailand, followed by another climb to altitude and a second penetration of North Vietnamese airspace made near the Demilitarised Zone (DMZ), after which he recovered the aircraft, after three instrument approaches in driving rain, back at Kadena. In all the flight had lasted three hours and 40 minutes. Several SA-2s were fired at the aircraft but all detonated above and well behind their target. The 'photo-take' was downloaded and sent by a special courier aircraft to the Eastman Kodak plant in Rochester, New York, for processing. '937's high resolution Type IV camera developed by Hycon had successfully photographed ten priority target categories, including 70 of the 190 known SAM sites. By mid-July, A-12 overflights had determined with a high degree of confidence that there were no surface-to-surface missiles in North Vietnam.

During a sortie flown by Denny Sullivan on 28 October 1967, he had indications on his Radar Homing Warning Receiver (RHWR), of almost continuous radar activity focused on his A-12, whilst both inbound and outbound over North Vietnam, which also included the launch of a single SA-2. Two days later he was again flying high over North Vietnam when two SAM sites tracked him on his first pass. On his second pass, approaching Hanoi from the East, he again noted he was being tracked on radar, Over the next few minutes he counted no less than eight SA-2 detonations in 'the general area, though none were particularly close'. After recovering the aircraft back at Kadena without further incident, a post-flight inspection revealed that a tiny piece of shrapnel had penetrated the lower wing fillet of his aircraft and become lodged against the support structure of the wing tank - this would prove to be the only occasion that a 'Blackbird' took 'a hit'.

Back at Area 51 the year ended with the loss of another A-12 when, on 28 December 1967, Mele Vojvodich took aircraft 60-6929 for a functional check flight (FCF) following a period of deep maintenance. On applying back pressure to the stick for rotation to lift-off, the aircraft's nose yawed viciously to one side. Mele attempted to correct the yaw with rudder, but this caused '929's nose to pitch-up. The rush of instinctive responses which followed resulted in a series of counter movements, completely opposite to those a pilot would expect to occur. Despite all the odds, Mele managed to get the aircraft to about 100ft, where he ejected after just

Above Evolution of the pressure suit continued throughout the Senior Crown programme. Here crew members undergoing water survival training are wearing chocolate brown S901 suits, with which some were equipped during the early 1970s. (Paul Crickmore)

Below Major Brian Shul gets suited up in his S1030 'gold suit'. (Paul Crickmore)

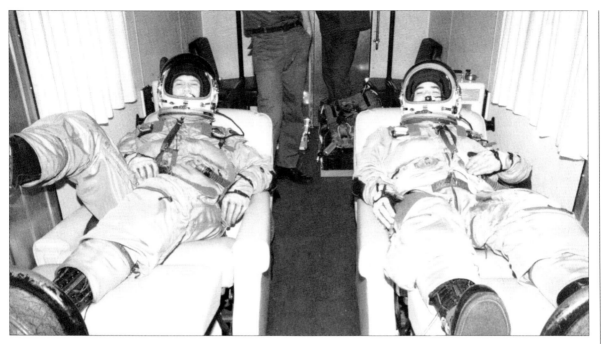

Above Pilot Maj Rich Judson and RSO Maj Frank Kelly are driven out to their waiting aircraft in the PSD van. (Paul Crickmore)

Below The S1030 suits cost $30,000 each, last between 10 and 12 years, undergo a complete overhaul every five years and a thorough inspection every 90 days or 150 hours. (Paul Crickmore)

six seconds of flight. Incredibly, he too survived and escaped serious injury. An accident investigation discovered that when the unit was re-installed following maintenance, the pitch Stability Augmentation System (SAS), had been connected to the yaw SAS actuators and vice-versa. Thereafter, the SAS connectors were changed to ensure incorrect wiring was impossible.

During 1967, a total of 41 A-12 missions were alerted, of which 22 were actually granted approval for flight. Between 1 January and 31 March 1968, 15 missions were alerted, of which only six were flown, four over North Vietnam and two over North Korea. The latter two came about as a result of the USS *Pueblo* - a US Navy Signal Intelligence (SIGINT) vessel being seized by North Korea during the night of 23 January. The first sortie was attempted by Jack Weeks on 25 January, but a malfunction on the A-12 resulted in an abort shortly after take off. The next day Frank Murray completed the task: "I left Kadena, topped-off, then entered northern airspace over the Sea of Japan via the Korean Straits. My first pass started off near Vladivostok, then with the camera on I flew down the east coast of North Korea where we thought the boat was. As I approached Wonsan I could see the *Pueblo* through my view sight. The harbour was all iced up except at the very entrance and there she was, sitting off to the right of the main entrance. I continued to the border with South Korea, completed a 180-degree turn and flew back over North Korea. I made four passes photographing the whole of North Korea from the DMZ to the Yalu border. As far as I know, I was undetected throughout the flight, but when I got back to Kadena some folks told me that the Chinese had detected me and told the North Koreans, but they never reacted." Back at Kadena 'the take' was immediately flown to Yakota AB, Japan where the 67th Reconnaissance Technical Squadron had been activated to enable the more timely exploitation of such data by theatre commanders.

On 8 May 1968, Jack Layton successfully completed the A-12's second mission over North Korea; it was to prove the final operational flight of an A-12. A long standing debate concerning whether the A-12 or a programme known as Senior Crown should carry forward the strategic reconnaissance baton, had, after three years, been resolved. Oxcart was vanquished. In early March 1968, SR-71s began arriving at Kadena to take over the Blackshield commitment. Those A-12s back at 'the Area' were flown to Palmdale and placed in storage by 7 June. At Kadena, the three aircraft that had performed all the Blackshield missions were also readied for a return transpacific ferry flight. On 2 June 1968 however, tragedy hit the Oxcart program a final blow, when Jack Weeks was killed during an FCF in 60-6932. The aircraft and its pilot were lost without trace in the Pacific Ocean. The two remaining A-12s on Okinawa, 60-6930 and 60-6937, were ferried back to Area 51, before being flown to Palmdale, the last flight being made by Frank Murray on 21 June 1968 in aircraft '937.

Tagboard & Senior Bowl

On 10 October 1962, Kelly Johnson received authorization from the CIA to carry out study work on a drone that would be mated with an A-12. At the root of such a request was the US Government's decision to discontinue overflight, following political fall-out after the Gary Powers shoot-down. Fourteen days later, Kelly, Ben Rich and Russ Daniell met representatives from Marquardt to discuss ramjet propulsion system options. Progress was rapid, on 7 December a full-scale mock-up of the craft was completed which was referred to within the Skunk Works as the Q-12. Still to receive mission specifications from the Agency, Kelly worked on producing a vehicle with a 3,000 n miles range hauling a Hycon camera system weighing 425 lbs and capable of a photographic

Top and Above To improve mission flexibility, the SR-71's nose section is detachable, enabling the aircraft to be fitted with a ground mapping radar unit or a 30 inch Optical Bar Camera (OBC) for horizon-to-horizon panoramic scanning. (Paul Crickmore).

Opposite, top The original nose radar unit, carried by the SR-71, housed a Goodyear PIP which was later replaced by the Loral CAPRE. This was finally replaced by the high resolution Advanced Synthetic Aperture Radar System (ASARS1), built again by Loral. This shot depicts the antenna belonging to the CAPRE system. (Lockheed Martin)

Right The right aft mission bay compartments Q and T revealed, into which a palletised 'close-look' or Technical Objective, TEOC camera can be loaded. (Paul Crickmore)

resolution of 6 inches from operating altitude. The engine to be used was the Marquardt RJ43 - MA-3 Bomarc, and by October 1963, the overall configuration for the Q-12 and its launch platforms - two purpose-built, modified A-12s - were nearing completion. Code-named 'Tagboard,' the designation of both elements was also changed, the carrier vehicle became the 'M' - standing for "Mother" - 21 and the Q-12 became the 'D - for "Daughter" - 21.

The 11,000lb D-21 was supported on the M-21 by a single, dorsally mounted pylon. Upon reaching launch point, the mothership's pilot maintained Mach 3.12 and initiated a 0.9 g push-over. Once released by the Launch Control Officer (LCO), sitting in what was, on other A-12 aircraft, the Q bay , the D-21 flew its sortie independently. Equipped with a Minneapolis-Honeywell inertial navigation system (INS), the D-21 would fly a pre-programmed flight profile, execute turns and camera on/off points to produce the perfect photo-recce sortie. Having completed its camera run, the drone's INS system then sent signals to the auto-pilot system to descend to a predetermined 'feet wet' film collection point. The entire palletised unit containing INS, camera and film was then ejected at 60,000 ft and Mach 1.67 and parachuted towards the ocean. As the drone continued its descent it was blown apart by a barometrically activated explosive charge. Meanwhile the air retrieval was executed by a JC-130B Hercules. On 12 August 1964, the first M-21 was dispatched to Groom Lake and on 22 December the first D-21/M-21 combination flight took place with Bill Park at the controls. Troubles however dogged Tagboard and it wasn't until 5 March that the first successful D-21 launch was accomplished. The second launch on 27 April saw the drone reach Mach 3.3, 90,000ft and fly for 1,200 n miles, holding course within half a mile throughout. The

Above A 'first generation' example of an enlarged OBC shot, taken by an SR-71 during a state-side training sortie whilst flying at Mach 3 and 80,000ft. Note the white lines delineating car parking spaces. (USAF)

Left An SR-71's TEOC, on its pallet, receives some maintenance - the shot was taken through a U-2's drift-sight. (USAF)

flight came to an end after a hydraulic pump burned out and the D-21 fell out of the sky.

The Air Force remained interested in the drone and on 29 April 1966, a second batch of D-21s were ordered. On 16 June a third successful launch was made and the D-21 flew 1,600 miles, completing all tasks on the flight card except ejecting the all important camera pallet. The fourth and final D-21 sortie from the M-21 occurred on 30 July 1966 and ended in disaster when the drone collided with '941 moments after achieving launch separation. The impact caused the mother craft to pitch up so violently that the fuselage forebody broke off. Both Bill Park and his LCO Ray Torick successfully ejected and made a 'feet wet' landing, but unfortunately Torick's pressure suit filled with water and he drowned before he could be rescued. Bill Park spent an hour in the ocean before he was brought aboard a US Navy vessel.

The D-21 was grounded for a year whilst a new launch system was developed. This new operation, code-named Senior Bowl, involved the drone being launched from the underwing pylons of two modified B-52Hs of the 4200th Test Wing based at Beale AFB. Upon launch the D-21B was accelerated to Mach 3.3 and 80,000ft by a solid propellant rocket developed by Lockheed Propulsion Company of Redlands, California. On achieving cruise speed and altitude the booster was jettisoned and the drone's flight continued as described earlier. The first launch attempt from a BUFF was made on 6 November 1967; this proved unsuccessful, as did three other attempts. Success was finally achieved on 16 June 1968. Between 9 November 1969 and 20 March 1971, a total of four operational flights over China were attempted. To maintain tight security the B-52, hauling its unique payload, departed Beale at night and lumbered westwards to the Pacific Island of Guam. Just before dawn the next day the flight resumed, the bomber departing Guam and

heading for the launch point. Upon vehicle separation, the Buff made its way back to Guam, while the D-21 embarked upon its pre-programmed day-time reconnaissance run. Achieving only limited success, Senior Bowl was cancelled on 15 July 1971.

Senior Crown

Whilst working on Oxcart back in the early spring of 1962, Kelly had mentioned the possibility of producing a reconnaissance/strike variant for the Air Force. Lockheed was duly issued with a 90-day study contract, wherein the various Air Force mission options were identified and defined in terms of the A-12 platform. By the end of April 1962, two different mock-ups were under construction referred to as the R-12 and RS-12. On 18 February

---

Below SR-71A 17964 undertook its first flight on 11 May 1966 with Lockheed test pilot Bill Weaver at the controls and Steve Belgau in the back seat. (Lockheed Martin)

Bottom The second 9th SRW aircraft to be lost was 17965, which crashed on 25 October 1967, Pilot, Maj Roy St Martin and his RSO Capt John Carnochan ejected safely. (Lockheed Martin)

1963, Lockheed received pre-contractual authority to build six aircraft, with the understanding that 25 aircraft would be ordered by 1 July. Col Leo Geary had been the RS-12's Weapon System Program Officer, but after protracted debate, it was decided that the A-12 project group under Col. Templeton, would inherit the R-12, which became designated SR-71 by the Air Force. The RS-12 and later the B-12/B71 proposals for a strike version of the aircraft would fail to win production contracts, despite Kelly having demonstrated to the Air Force the unique capabilities of such a platform. This was largely due to the far greater lobbying powers of the XB-70 and later the FB-111 fraternity. During a speech made on 24 July 1964, President Johnson revealed to the world the existence of the SR-71.

In August, Kelly phoned Bob Murphy and asked him if he wanted to work on the SR-71 programme. At the time, Murphy was a superintendent in charge of D-21 drone production. Drone number one was undergoing final check-out while nine others were at various stages of assembly. Bob accepted the offer and was immediately briefed by Kelly: "I want you to go to Palmdale and get site 2 away from Rockwell". This achieved, the prototype SR-71A, serial 64-17950 (article number 2001), was delivered from Burbank to Site 2, Air Force Plant 42, Building 210, at Palmdale for final assembly on 29 October, by two large trailers specifically designed for the task. Earlier that year, Kelly had promoted the charismat-

ic Robert J Gilliland to the position of chief project pilot for the SR-71, a post for which Bob was admirably qualified, having gained a great deal of experience as a member of the F-104 and A-12 test teams.

With two J-58s installed, '950 conducted its first engine test run on 18 December 1964. Three days later, a 'non-flight' was completed, where Gilliland accelerated the aircraft to 120kts before snapping the throttles back to idle and deploying the large 40-feet drag chute. On 22 December 1964, Gilliland, using his personal callsign 'Dutch 51' successfully completed the first flight of an SR-71A in prototype 64-17950 – Article 2001 (the significance of this number being that it was the date Kelly

Below SR-71 17955 was operated extensively by Air Force Logistics Command from Plant 42, Palmdale and was dedicated SR-71 test aircraft. It is seen here in company with a U-2R. (Lockheed Martin)

Above To celebrate America's Bi-Centennial, several record breaking flights were made by SR-71s which had a large white cross applied to their underside to assist ground based tracking cameras. Here 17958 returns to earth. (Lockheed Martin)

believed would be reached before the aircraft became vulnerable to interception).

Aircraft 951 and 952 were added to the test fleet for contractor development of payload systems and techniques and shortly after the phase II, Developmental Test Programme was started, four other Lockheed test pilots were brought into the project: Jim Eastham, Bill Weaver, Art Peterson and Darrell Greenamyer.

Developmental efforts within Lockheed were matched by Air Force Systems Command (AFSC) where Col Ben Bellis had been appointed the SR-71 System Programme Officer (SPO). His task was to structure a 'Development and Evaluation Programme' that would evaluate the new aircraft for the Air Force, a program undertaken by the SR-71/YF12 Test Force, located at the Air Force Flight Test Centre, Edwards AFB. Both Phase 1 'Experimental' and phase II 'Development' test flying had moved to Edwards where SR-71As 953, 954, and 955 were to be used by the 'blue suiters'. However, the SR-71s were plagued by problems associated with the electrical system, tank sealing and difficulties in obtaining design range.

Whilst these problems were being worked at, Beale AFB, chosen home for the newcomer, had been undergoing an $8.4 million construction program which included the installation of an army of specialised technical support facilities. The 4200th Strategic Reconnaissance Wing was activated at Beale on 1 January 1965 and three months later, four support squadrons were formed. In January 1966, Col Doug Nelson was appointed commander of the new wing - a job for which he was eminently qualified, having been the Director of Operations for the Oxcart project. Doug began by selecting a small group of highly competent sub-commanders and Strategic Air Command (SAC) fliers to form the initial cadre of the SR-71 unit.

Bottom Due to high airframe temperatures when cruising at Mach 3.2, a special flash resistant fuel was developed. Known as JP-7, normal fuel igniters are unable to generate the heat required to set fuel burning during start-up or when engaging the afterburners. A chemical ignition system (CIS) was therefore developed using Triethylborane (TEB), which ignites with a green flash. (Paul Crickmore)

Below With both 'burners' engaged, SR-71A serial 17960, call-sign TRULY55 starts to roll down RAF Mildenhall's runway. (Paul Crickmore)

Above Standard operating procedures call for the SR-71 to get airborne with a light fuel load, enabling it to land back immediately should a problem develop. Once airborne, the first order of business is to 'hook-up' with the tanker and top-off with fuel. (Paul Crickmore)

Right Prior to boom conect, the aircraft establishes itself in the pre-contact position. (Paul Crickmore)

Col Bill Hayes became the deputy commander for maintenance, Lt Col Ray Haupt, Chief Instructor Pilot, Col Walt Wright commanded the Medical Group, Col Clyde Deaniston supervised all category III flight test planning and the flight crews were recruited from the best SAC bomber pilots and navigators in the service.

The first two of eight Northrop T-38 Talons arrived at Beale on 7 July 1965, to be used as 'companion trainers' to maintain overall flying proficiency for the SR-71 crew at a fraction of the cost of flying the main aircraft.

On 7 January 1966, Col Doug Nelson and his Chief Instructor, Lt Col Ray Haupt delivered the first SR-71B to Beale AFB. Five months later, on 14 April, Nelson and Maj Al Pennington took delivery of Beale's first SR-71A, serial 64-17958. On 25 June 1966, the 4200th was redesignated the 9th Strategic Reconnaissance Wing (SRW) its component flying squadrons being the 1st and 99th Strategic Reconnaissance Squadrons (SRS). Crew training and Category III Operational Testing then proceeded in earnest.

Losses

Progress came at a heavy price. The first SR-71 loss occurred on 25 January 1966, when Bill Weaver and his test engineer Jim Zwayer took off from Edwards in SR-71A '952. After in-flight refuelling, 'Dutch 64' climbed back to cruising altitude. While in a 15-degree right back turn, manually controlling the right forward bypass doors at Mach 3.17 and between 77-78,000ft, Weaver experi-

enced a right inlet unstart. Bank angle immediately increased from 35 to 60 degrees and the aircraft entered a pitch-up that exceeded the restorative authority of the flight controls and SAS. The aircraft disintegrated, but miraculously Weaver survived; unfortunately Jim Zwayer was killed in the incident.

The SR-71 prototype was written off on 10 January 1967, during an anti-skid brake system evaluation at Edwards AFB, the Lockheed test pilot Art Peterson escaped with a cracked disc in his back. Three months later, on 13 April, Beale lost SR-71A '966 flown by Capts Earle Boone and RSO Butch Sheffield following a stall and pitch-up. Both men safely ejected as '966 made its

Above Once on the boom, the pilot formates with the tanker, whilst the boom operator maintains contact and the tanker's co-pilot supervises the fuel off-load. (Paul Crickmore)

Top SR-71s refuelled from both KC-135 and KC-10 Tankers. (Lockheed Martin)

Above right Once disconnected from the boom, the SR-71 side-slips clear of the tanker, engages both 'burners' and accelerates away. (Paul Crickmore)

grave not far from that of Bill Weaver's aircraft, in Northern New Mexico.

On the night of 25 October 1967, Maj Roy St Martin and Capt John Carnochan were flying a night sortie in aircraft '965. As Roy eased the aircraft into the descent profile over Nevada, the gyro-stabilised reference platform for the ANS drifted without a failure warning. With no visual horizon for external reference, the aircraft rolled over, the nose fell far below a safe descent angle and plunged through 60,000ft. Sensing something was wrong, Roy glanced at the standby artificial horizon and was alarmed to see it indicate a 'screaming dive and roll-over toward inverted flight'. He attempted a 'recovery from

63

Above Depending upon time and fuel remaining, a returning aircraft might shoot a few approaches before recovery. Here ex-Thunderbirds pilot Maj Jim Jiggens demonstrates the more nimble side of 17960. (Paul Crickmore)

unusual positions manoeuvre', and managed to roll the wings level, but roaring through 40,000ft, well above the speed from which level flight could be achieved, both men ejected. The RSO went first, and as Roy ejected he heard the warning horn that signalled that the aircraft had descended below 10,000ft! Aircraft 965 plunged into the ground near Lovelock, Nevada like a meteorite. Luckily both men survived without permanent injuries and following an accident board of investigation several instrumentation changes were implemented on the fleet, together with an amended training program containing less night flying until crews had accumulated more daytime experience in the SR-71.

As mentioned earlier, with both the Air Force and Agency operating similar aircraft in the same role, a Bureau of the Budget (BoB) memo, dated November 1965, questioned such a requirement. Since the SR-71 was not scheduled to become operational until September 1968, the SECDEF rightly declined to consider any cut-backs. In July 1966, BoB officials proposed that a tri-agency study be set up again to establish ways of reducing the cost of both programs. After the study was completed, a meeting was convened on 12 December 1966 and a vote taken on available options. Three out of four votes cast were in favour of the recommendation to 'terminate the Oxcart fleet in January 1968 (assuming an operational readiness date of September 1967 for the SR-71) and assign all missions to the SR-71 fleet'. The BoB memorandum was transmitted to President Johnson on 16 December, despite protestations from the CIA's Richard Helms, who was the sole dissenting voice in the vote. Twelve days later, Johnson accepted the BoB's recommendations and directed that the Oxcart programme be terminated by 1 January 1968. In the event, the Oxcart run-down lagged, but the original decision to terminate

Middle and above Normal approach speed (dependent upon weight, ambient air temperature etc) is 175 kts with ten degrees of nose up pitch. Final flare further increases alpha-nose up pitch and speed reduces to 155 kts for touch down. A strong ground effect, produced by the delta wing, cushions landings. (Paul Crickmore)

the program was reaffirmed on 16 May 1968 and the first Kadena-based A-12 began its flight back to the States on 7 June.

Preparations for Deployment

As the 9th SRW prepared to deploy overseas, much talk in the crew lounge was devoted to anti-SAM tactics. The plan was to penetrate enemy airspace at Mach 3; if fired upon, the pilot would accelerate to Mach 3.2 and climb, thereby forcing the missile's guidance system to recalculate the intercept equation. One half-baked idea was to dump fuel at the same time, thereby becoming lighter and increasing the rate of climb. The debate was ended during a training sortie over Montana, when a crew dumped fuel for ten seconds to see if the afterburner would ignite the fuel trail. Instead it turned instantly into an ice cloud in the -55 degree stratosphere and left a five mile-long contrail - finger pointing directly to the aircraft. The pilot reported that he could see the trail for hundreds of miles after having turned back towards the west!

On 11 January 1968, during this work-up period, yet another incident befell the 9th SRW. Lt Col 'Gray' Sowers and 'student' Capt Dave Fuehauf - on his third training sortie - experienced a double generator failure in SR-71B '957, near Spokane, Washington. They immediately switched off all non-essential electrically powered equipment to conserve battery power and despite repeated attempts they were unable to re-set both generators. With most of Washington State bases weathered out, they had little option but to press on for Beale. Their long straight in approach looked good until the 175kts 'final' placed the aircraft in its natural ten degrees nose-up angle of attack. This allowed some dry-tank fuel inlet ports to 'suck air' which in turn interrupted the gravity flow of fuel to the engine combustion chambers, because the fuel boost pumps were inoperative. This caused cavitation, both J58s flamed out and at 3,000ft Gray ordered bail-out. Both crew members survived as '957 'pancaked' inverted, only seven miles north of Beale's long runway.

Above On landing, a forty-foot diameter brake chute rapidly decelerates the aircraft. (Paul Crickmore)

Below Back in 'the barn' the crew disembark and are driven back to the Physiological Support Division (PSD) building where they shower and change before debriefing the mission. (Paul Crickmore)

OL-8

As the 1 SRS neared operational readiness, decisions were made by Col Bill Hayes (9th SRW Commander) and Col Hal Confer (Director of Operations) as to which crews would be first to be deployed to Kadena AB, Okinawa. Three aircraft and four crews would be deployed and the crews themselves pulled straws to decide the 'batting order'; the fourth crew would be standby for the three deploying aircraft and would arrive on Kadena, if their services weren't needed, by KC-135Q tanker. Command of the Operating Location (OL-8) would alternate between the 9th SRW's wing commander and vice commander (and later Deputy Chief of Operations). Two days before Glowing Heat, the codename for the deployment, six KC-135Q tankers were positioned at Hickam AFB, Hawaii. Emergency radio coverage was set up on Wake Island and on 8th March 1968, Majs Buddy Brown and his RSO Dave Jenson left Beale in '978 and became the first Senior Crown crew to deploy to Kadena. Two

days later Maj Jerry O'Malley and Capt Ed Payne delivered '976 to the OL, to be followed on the 13 March by Bob Spencer and Keith Branham in '974. Finally, three days later, in late evening rain Jim Watkins and Dave Dempster the back-up crew, were wearily disgorged from the '135. The crews and their mounts were ready for business.

Due to maintenance problems, Buddy Brown and Dave Jenson missed their chance of being the first crew to fly the SR-71 operationally; instead, that accolade went to Maj Jerry O'Malley and Capt Ed Payne in '976. The

Below Two SR-71B pilot trainers were built, serials 17956 and 17957. (USAF)

Bottom SR-71B, 17957 crashed on 11 January 1968, both the IP Lt Col 'Gray' Sowers and the student Capt Dave Fruehauf ejected safely. (Appeal Democrat)

mission was flown on Thursday 21 March 1968 and their route was similar to that flown by Mele Vojvodich in his A-12 ten months earlier. However, with its large, high definition camera in the Q bay, the A-12 was a photographic platform only. For its first operational mission, the SR-71 carried both cameras and Goodyear Side-Looking Airborne Radar (SLAR) located in a detachable nose section, together with its associated AR-1700 radar recorder unit.

Having refuelled after their first run, Jerry climbed and accelerated on track for their final 'take' for the mission, which was to be flown over the DMZ. For this run, the primary sensor was the SLAR. On arrival back at Kadena Jerry and Ed were confronted with a base completely 'fogged in'. Despite a good Ground Controlled Approach (GCA), Jerry never saw the runway and climbed back to contemplate further options. Low on fuel, another tanker was launched and 25,000lbs of fuel taken onboard. The crew then received a two-figure encoded number which told them to divert to Taiwan. In company with two tankers and the SR-71 adopting a tanker call-sign for security reasons, the three ship formation made its slow, lumbering way to Ching Chuan Kang, Taiwan. On arrival the SR-71 was quickly hangared and the next day the 'take' was downloaded and despatched for processing – the film to the 67th RTS at Yokota AB, Japan and the SLAR imagery to the 9RTS at Beale AFB. After two nights at CCK, Jerry and Ed ferried '976 back to Kadena and a superb reception from their friends.

Post-mission intelligence results were stunning. The SLAR imagery had revealed the location of many artillery emplacements around Khe Sanh, and a huge truck park used for logistics support. These sites had eluded US sensors on other recce aircraft up to that point. Over the next few days air strikes were mounted against both targets, reducing their effectiveness dramatically. After a 77 day siege, Khe Sanh was at last relieved on 7 April 1968 (two weeks after '976's discovery sortie). As a result of their highly successful mission both Maj Jerome F O'Malley and Capt Edward D Payne were each awarded the Distinguished Flying Cross. On its very first operational mission the SR-71 had proved its value.

Above The raised cockpit of SR-71B 17956 is immediately apparent as this aircraft taxies back - note brake chute doors open. (Paul Crickmore)

Below To compensate for the loss of 17957, YF-12A 60-6934 was taken from storage and its front forebody replaced by a static test specimen to create the so-called SR-71C, which was re-serialed 17981 and nicknamed 'The Bastard'. (USAF)

Early OL-8 operational sorties were typified by problems involving the SR-71's generators, this often led to aircraft having to divert into one of the USAF bases in Thailand. Of the 168 SR-71 sorties flown by OL-8 throughout 1968, 67 were operational missions over North Vietnam, the remaining sorties being FCFs or for crew training. In addition the first of many aircraft change arounds took place when over a period of seven days in September, '970 and '962 took over from '978, '976 and '974. Crew rotation also took place with no less than 21 crews having taken the SR-71 into battle over the same period. It was while operating out of Kadena that the SR-71 received its nickname, Habu, after a poisonous pit viper found on the Ryuku Islands: though non aggressive, it can inflict a painful bite if provoked. Although resisted by officialdom, the name Habu proved to be ineradicable amongst all associated with Senior Crown.

OL-8 lost its first 'Habu' on 10 May 1970, shortly after Majs Willie Lawson and Gil Mortinez had air refuelled '969 near Korat RTAFB. Struggling to clear a saddle-back of cloud at 30,000ft, Lawson eased '969 into a slightly steeper climb. However, on entering turbulent cloud, both engines flamed out. The aircraft's angle of attack increased, then suddenly the nose pitched-up and recovery was impossible. Both crew members ejected safely and landed, resplendent in their 'silver moon suits', near U Tapao.

Other Sorties

Although the vast majority of early Habu flights from Kadena were in support operations in Vietnam, this was not exclusively the case. On the night of 27 September 1971, Majs Bob Spencer and 'Butch' Sheffield flew '980 on a northerly track. US Intelligence had obtained details of the largest ever Soviet naval exercise to be held off Vladivostok, in the Sea of Japan; and the Habu was an ideal vehicle for stirring up the Soviet fleet's defence systems. National security officials were especially interested in obtaining signal details relating to the Soviets' new SA-5 (Gammon) SAM system.

As '980 bore down on the target area, dozens of Soviet radars were switched on and just short of entering Soviet airspace, the Habu was rolled into a full 35 degree banked turn, remaining throughout in international airspace. However, on approach to the collection area, Bob noted the right engine's oil pressure was dropping. Clearing the

area, Bob discovered the reading had fallen to zero. He shut down the engine and was forced to descend and decelerate to subsonic speeds. Having stirred up a hornets nest, they were now sitting ducks for any Soviet fast jets sent up to intercept the oil-starved Habu. Worse still, at lower altitude they were subjected to strong headwinds which rapidly depleted their fuel supply. Butch calculated that recovery back to Kadena was impossible - instead they'd have to divert into South Korea.

The OL commander had been monitoring '980's slow progress and as the Habu neared Korea, US listening posts reported the launch of several MiGs from

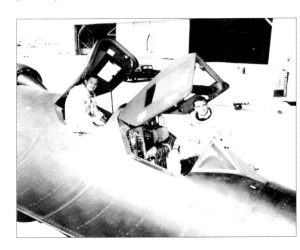

Above and below Majs Jerry O'Malley and RSO Ed Payne flew the first operational SR-71 sortie over North Vietnam in 17976 on Thursday 21 March 1968. (USAF/Lindsay Peacock)

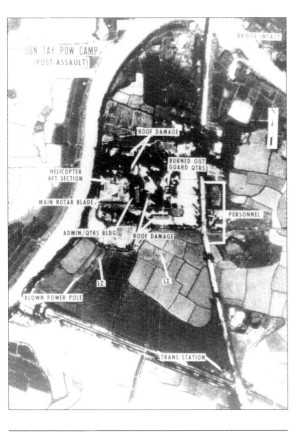

Above This shot was taken by an SR-71 following the failed attempt by US Special Forces to liberate POWs held by the North Vietnamese in Son Tay camp. (USAF)

Pyongyang, North Korea. In response USAF F-102s were scrambled from a base near Hon Chew, South Korea and vectored into a position between the Habu and the MiGs. It was later established that the MiG launch was unconnected with the Habu's descent and Bob recovered '980 into Taegu, South Korea, without further incident. In all their EMR 'take' had recorded emissions from 290 different radars, but the greatest prize was 'capture' of the much sought-after SA-5 signal characteristics.

On 20 July 1972 while returning to Kadena from an operational mission, Majs Denny Bush and Jimmy Fagg were caught shortly after touch down in '978 by excessive cross winds. Jettisoning the 'chute by the book, to prevent the aircraft from 'weather-cocking' sharply into wind, the extended roll-out caused the aircraft to roll off the end of the runway and in a twist of fate, they hit the concrete housing for emergency crash barriers. One of the main landing gear struts was badly damaged which in turn caused substantial additional damage. Both crew members were unhurt, but '978 was written off. The final SR-71 to be written off was lost on 21 April 1989. On that occasion one of the engine compressor discs disintegrated during Mach 3 flight, the debris severing one hydraulic system and damaging the other. Lt Col Dan House and Maj Blair Bozek decelerated and descended '974 down to 400kts and 10,000ft. When the remaining hydraulic system ran dry, both men safely ejected just a few hundred yards off the coast of Luzon and were picked up by Philippino fishermen. They were later collected by an HH-53 Super Jolly Green Giant and flown to Clark AFB.

OL-8 was redesignated OL RK on 30 October 1970, became OL KA on 26 October 1971 finally Detachment 1 or Det 1, of the 9th SRW in August 1974, a title it retained until deactivated in 1990. During 22 years of service, the unit flew missions to Vietnam, Laos, Cambodia, Thailand, North Korea, airspace off the USSR, China and four 11-hour return flights to the Persian Gulf, during the Iran/Iraq war.

Operations from the USA

Rolling down Beale's runway 14, in '977, on October 1968, new pilot/RSO team Majs Abe Kardong and Jim Kogler were approaching V1 when a wheel failed, throwing shrapnel into the fuel cells and causing a fuel fire. Abe aborted take-off at high speed, causing the remaining tyres on that leg to burst. The brake 'chute blossomed only to be consumed immediately by the fire. With one wing low and the aircraft off-centre to the runway, '977's sharp inlet spike knifed through the barrier cable at the end of the runway, rendering it useless. Now on the overrun, Jim ejected while Abe rode out the high-speed sleigh ride. When the dust settled, he was helped from the cockpit by the Mobile Control crew for that day, Willie Lawson and Gil Martinez. Despite four 9th SRW aircraft losses between 13 April 1967 and 10 October 1968, Category III 'Operational' Testing ended in December 1968 and the wing was awarded the Presidential Unit Citation for meeting the challenges of bringing the most advanced reconnaissance system of its day to operational readiness.

On 11 April 1969, Lt Col Bill Skliar and Maj Noel Warner lost SR-71A, 64-17953 on the Edwards runway

Above Darrell Greenamyer and Steve Belgau first flew the 'Big Tail' conversion of 17959 on 11 December 1975. The redesign increased reconnaissance gathering capacity but was not pursued on the operational fleet. (Paul Crickmore Collection)

Left The last operational SR-71 to be lost was 17974 on 21 April 1989. Pilot Maj Dan House and his RSO Capt Blair Bozek ejected safely. (Paul Crickmore Collection)

Right Detachment 4 (Det 4) of the 9th SRW was created at RAF Mildenhall on 1 April 1979. (Paul Crickmore)

Bottom right Another Det 4 sortie gets underway. (Paul Crickmore)

following an incident similar to the loss of '977. 'Dutch 69' had just rotated when one of the left main gear tyres blew. With the aircraft at max gross weight, the other two tyres on that leg also blew. Bill aborted the take-off, but red hot shrapnel from the disintegrating wheel hubs punctured the fuel tanks and triggered a fire which engulfed the entire aircraft. Once at a standstill Bill exited the aircraft to the right and assisted Noel from his rear cockpit. '953 never flew again and after this accident the Goodrich tyres were 'beefed up'.

A third pitch-up accident happened on 18 December 1969, when Director of the Test Force, Lt Col Joe Rogers and RSO Lt Col Gary Heidelbaugh were accelerating and climbing '953. They heard a loud explosion which was accompanied by a loss of power and severe

control difficulties. As the aircraft decelerated, its angle of attack continued to increase, despite Joe 'firewalling' the control stick. Realising they'd entered an irrecoverable corner of the flight envelope, ten seconds after the explosion, Joe ordered "Let's get out Gary" and both men safely ejected; '953 crashed at the Southern end of Death Valley. The cause of the explosion remains unknown.

On 17 June 1970, the 9th lost another SR-71A, serial '970, following a mid-air collision with a KC-135Q shortly after taking aboard 35,000 lbs of fuel. The Habu hit clear air turbulence (CAT) and the entire nose of the aircraft smashed into the rear of the tanker. No one aboard the tanker was injured and Buddy Brown and Mort Jarvis were able to eject safely - although the former sustained two broken legs during the ejection.

At 1400hrs on 6 October 1973, Syrian and Egyptian artillery barrages on the state of Israel spelled the beginning of the Yom Kippur War. With Israel caught off guard, the Arabs made substantial gains both in the Sinai and the Golan Heights. In view of the grave situation faced by Israel, the US decided to step up intelligence efforts and used the SR-71 to provide a hot-spot reconnaissance capability. CINC SAC General John Meyer ordered Col Pat Halloran (9th SRW Commander) to prepare for missions that would be flown from Beale across the war zone and recover into RAF Mildenhall, England. However, the Heath government denied the SR-71's use of Mildenhall in a move designed to safeguard the supply of Arab oil to the United Kingdom.

Instead, round-robin missions would be flown from Griffiss AFB, New York; accordingly, two SR-71As, '979 and '964, were despatched to the east coast air base where they arrived on 12 October. At 0600 a secure teleprinter clattered out details of the first sortie which was to be flown just 22 hours later. The belligerent attitude of usually helpful allies necessitated that JP 7 fuel and tanker crews be re-positioned from Mildenhall and Turkey to Zargoza in Spain and emergency landing sites were proving all but impossible to find. Nevertheless, Jim Shelton cranked '979's engines on cue and lifted off from Griffiss and headed east at 0200hrs. Just off the east coast he made good the first of many ARCP's (Air Refuelling Contact Points), he topped-off and continued east to the

next cell of tankers awaiting the thirsty Habu just beyond the Azores. Returning again to speed and altitude they made a high-Mach dash through the Straits of Gibraltar and let-down for a third air refuelling just east of the heel of Italy. Due to its proximity to the war zone and Libya, the US Navy provided a CAP (Combat Air Patrol), from carrier-based aircraft on station in the Mediterranean. They then climbed and accelerated to coast-in over Port Said. Gary Coleman, the RSO: "There was no indication that anything launched against us, but everyone was painting us on their radars as we made our turn inbound. The DEF panel lit up like a pin-ball machine and I said to Jim, 'this should be interesting.'" In all '979 spent 25 minutes over 'denied territory'. Entering Egyptian airspace at 1103 GMT, they covered the Israeli battle fronts with both Egypt and Syria before coasting out and letting down towards their fourth ARCP, which was still being capped by the US Navy. Their next hot leg was punctuated by a fifth refuelling, again near the Azores, before a final high-speed run across the western Atlantic towards New York. Mindful of his own fatigue, Gary was in awe of his pilot who completed a text book sixth air refuelling, before greasing '979 back down at Griffiss after a combat sortie lasting ten hours eighteen minutes (more than five hours of which was at Mach 3 or above) and involving eleven tanking operations from the ever dependable KC-135Qs. Their reconnaissance 'take' was of high quality and provided intelligence and defense analysts with much needed information concerning the deposition of Arab forces in the region, which was then made available to the Israelis.

Aircraft '979 paid a second successful visit to the Yom Kippur war zone on 25 October, this time being crewed by Majs Al Joerz and John Fuller. A third mission was chalked up by the same aircraft eight days later. Majs Jim Wilson and Bruce Douglas took' 964 on its first sortie to the Mediterranean on 11 November. The ten hour 49-

minute flight departed Griffiss and terminated as planned at Seymour Johnson AFB, North Carolina, where the detachment had migrated to avoid the New York winter weather.

Despite hostilities between the factions officially ending with a Soviet-backed motion in the United Nations on 24 October, fierce fire-fighting continue to break out at regular intervals and it was to cover disengagement that the SR-71's monitoring system continued to be called upon, with five further marathon flights being flown from Seymour Johnson AFB.

In total, these nine flights represent a pinnacle of operational professionalism and serve as a tribute, not only to the dedication of the aircrews, but also to that of the staff planners, tanker crews and of course the unsung heroes, that small group of top ground technicians who maintained the SR-71s away from home. The sorties also stand as a testament to the long-reach capability of the aircraft and its ability to operate, on short notice, with impunity in a high threat environment.

Cuba

Early in the Senior Crown Programme, Cuban reconnaissance sorties became a task for the 9th SRW. Flown from Beale and initially code-named Giant Plate, the designation was later changed to 'Clipper'. Most sorties were 'stand-off' runs, flown abeam the island in international airspace. Such a mission would typically take three and a half hours to complete and was considered very routine. Occasionally however, the track was modified to take the aircraft directly over Cuba. When the Carter administration entered office, they suspended all overflight actively in an act of 'goodwill'. In 1978 however, a reconnaissance satellite photographed a Soviet freighter in Havana harbour surrounded by large crates that were being moved to a nearby air base where aircraft were being reassembled. It appeared that 15 MiG-23s had been supplied to Castro's Air Force. The MiG-23BN Flogger H Model was known to be capable of carrying nuclear weapons and if it was this variant that had been exported, then the shipment violated the 1962 Soviet pledge not to deploy 'offensive' weapons on Cuba. Two sorties were flown by SR-71s over Cuba in November 1978. These verified that

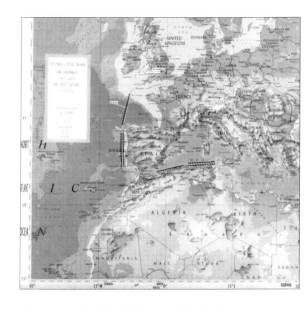

Above Map used by Secretary of Defence Casper Weinberger at a White House briefing shows route details of Operation Eldorado Canyon, the US strike at Libya on 15 April 1986. (DoD)

Below Lt Cols Jerry Glasser and RSO Ron Tabor return 17980, callsign Tromp 30, back to Mildenhall following the successful completion of their Bomb Damage Assessment (BDA) flight. (Paul Crickmore Collection)

Opposite above After the raid, some degraded shots were released to the press. Although never officially acknowledged, they originated from the SR-71's camera system. (DoD)

Opposite, bottom Just before 17980 returned to the US on completion of its TDY stint at Det 4, three dark red camel emblems were applied to the left nose gear door, in recognition of its part in the Eldorado Canyon sorties. (Paul Crickmore)

BENINA AIRFIELD
15 APR 86

DESTROYED F-27

DAMAGED MI-8/HIP

DESTROYED MI-8/HIP

they were in fact MiG-23Ms Flogger Es, optimised for air defence; evidence which substantiated Soviet claims.

Det 4, Mildenhall

Not long into Senior Crown, the total number of operatial SR-71s was scaled down. The two flying squadrons became one in April 1971. Then as the US disengaged itself from Vietnam, the number of unit-authorised aircraft also declined. By 1977, the number of SR-71A Primary Authorised Aircraft (PAA) stood at six and funding was reduced proportionately. Despite being tasked by national agencies to support a variety of theatre intelligence requirements, this extremely expensive aircraft operation was funded by the Air Force. HQ SAC were hostile to Senior Crown because it diverted funds away from its bomber and tanker mission and national intelligence agencies had become enamoured with satellite generated products. SAC's Single Integrated Operational Plan (SIOP), for the unthinkable needed SIGINT to keep it up to date, and the SR-71 wasn't capable of gathering 'long-on-station' samples of SIGINT like the RC-135s and U-2Rs. The loss of its SAC patronage left Senior Crown increasingly isolated and vulnerable. To survive

continued budgetary raids, it was apparent that the SR-71's utility had to be improved in order to become competitive with overhead systems. This required an updated sensor package, particularly an air-to-ground data link system coupled to its Synthetic Aperture Radar.

A 'marketing package' was assembled which included details of the SR-71's performance and imagery capabilities. In the mid-seventies, Senior Crown advocates embarked on a PR campaign within the Washington intelligence community to gather support for the program. Following a briefing to intelligence officers of the Navy's Atlantic fleet, interest was expressed in the SR-71's sea-scanning radar capabilities to detect submarines in their home ports in the Baltic and Arctic areas. The possibility existed that a new requirement could arise which would give Senior Crown a second lease of life. Two missions were flown over the Soviet Pacific fleet near Vladivostok to test the concept and the results were impressive.

Eighteen months after aircraft '972 had established a new transatlantic world speed record, the same aircraft returned to England and flew two aborted missions in a bid to obtain SLAR imagery of the Soviet Northern fleet. The ten-day deployment was an intelligence gathering failure, however important lessons were learned about aircraft operating procedures in Arctic air masses.

Aircraft '962 arrived during Exercise Teamwork on 6 September 1976, and flew the very next day on a 'Barents Sea Mission' codenamed Coldfire 001. Majs Rich Graham and Don Emmons flew that and another round-robin sortie out of RAF Mildenhall, Suffolk, before returning '962 to Beale on 18 September. The SR-71's SLAR and camera systems 'to gather simultaneous, synoptic coverage' of the Soviet submarine fleet based on the Kolskiy Polustrov, in Murmansk and bases on the Baltic had been validated. After nearly two years of short TDY deployments, Detachment 4 (Det 4) of the 9th SRW was activated and two SR-71s were permanently based at RAF Mildenhall.

Above All battened down and ready for a mission, the crew of 17964 awaits signals from a ground marshal in December 1987. (Paul Crickmore)

Opposite, top 17962 formates with two RAF Jaguars of 41 Recce Squadron, based at RAF Coltishall. (Crown Copyright)

Below 17980 at the RAF Mildenhall Airshow. (Paul Crickmore)

Yemen

During the early spring of 1979, tensions between Saudi Arabia and the People's Republic of Yemen were strained to the point where the US intelligence community believed that the Republic was on the brink of invading its northern neighbour. As a result, on the morning of Monday 12 March, Majs Rich Graham and Don Emmons deployed 972 from Beale to Det4 inorder to furnish decision makers with the necessary intelligence information.

After two early morning ground aborts due to cloud cover over the 'collection area', the mission finally got underway. Buzz Carpenter and his RSO, John Murphy got airborne and headed for their ARCP off Lands' End. Unfortunately, Buzz suffered a violent attack of diarrhoea while on the tanker boom, but despite his discomfort, he elected to continue the mission. Having completed the full fuel off-load they accelerated due south; since France had denied them the right to overfly, it was necessary to skirt the Iberian peninsula, entering the Mediterranean Sea through the Straits of Gibraltar. They then completed a second refuelling before returning to high Mach flight and overflying the Suez Canal, before a third tanker rendezvous over the Red Sea. The planned double-loop coverage of the collection area was interrupted by the ANS, which tried to initiate a pre-programmed turn prior to reaching the correct destination point (DP). Recognising the error, the crew flew the aeroplane manually while trying to work out what had caused the AUTONAV 'glitch'. As a result of the miscue, they overshot the turn point, but completed the rest of the route and made their way back to the tankers for another Red Sea top-up. A fifth air refuelling was completed east of Gibraltar and an hour-and-a-half later they recovered '972 back to Mildenhall after a full ten-hour mission.

This mission had generated considerable interest within the 9th SRW as well as at SAC Headquarters and in Washington. As a result, Buzz and John were greeted by a large number of their colleagues as they stepped off the gantry (including Col Dave Young, the 9th SRW vice commander), who presented Buzz with a brown SR-71 tie tack to commemorate the in-flight incident when, to misquote a well known phrase, 'the world fell out of Buzz's bottom'.

When the 'take' was processed, it was of exceptional quality and the incident which had delayed their turn had yielded the most important information. That unexpected success made additional flights to the area unnecessary.

Consequently, Rich Graham and Don Emmons returned 972 to Beale on 28 March. Deployments to Suffolk continued throughout the early eighties, the main 'collection areas' being the Barents and Baltic, in support of US Navy intelligence requirements. On 9 July 1983, British aviation enthusiasts 'manning' the many off-base vantage points of Mildenhall noted the arrival of aircraft '962, an aircraft that had 'pulled' TDY at the base on previous occasions. In fact Majs Maury Rosenberg and 'ED' McKim had just completed a seven hour operational flight from Beale to Mildenhall via the Barents/Baltic areas in the Palmdale flight test aircraft '955. The false serial number had been applied to ensure unwelcome attention was not drawn to the unique operational test deployment then underway.

In its detachable nose section, '955 was equipped with Loral's Advanced Synthetic Radar System (ASARS-1), a system that provided a quantum leap in radar resolution. With maritime data collected during the inbound flight, Majs 'BC' Thomas and John Morgan conducted a 2.6 hr ASARS operational test sortie of land-based targets in East Germany nine days later. On 21 July, Maury and ED took their turn on a four hour mission. The final ASARS operational proving flight was conducted by BC and John on 30 July, when they flew '962, ie '955, on a 7.3 hr flight back to Beale, again via the Baltic and Barents Seas. The series of tests were extremely successful and following further tests back at Palmdale, two production radar sets for the operational fleet were funded and deployed.

Eldorado Canyon

Tension between the United States and much of the Arab world continued, and after a series of incidents, President Reagan's patience came to a violent end. On 15 April 1986, operation Eldorado Canyon, a coordinated strike on targets in Libya, by air elements of the US Navy and

eighteen USAF F-111s from RAF Lakenheath, was mounted. Lt Cols Jerry Glasser and Ron Tabor took off from Mildenhall as scheduled at 0500 hrs in SR-71 '980 (callsign Tromp 30). Their mission was to secure photographic imagery for post-strike bomb damage assessment (BDA). To achieve this it would be necessary to overfly targets hit earlier, but this time in broad daylight and with the sophisticated Libyan defence network on full alert. Such was the importance of the mission that SR-71A 960 (Tromp 31) flown by Majs Brian Shul and Walt Watson, launched at 0615 hrs as an airborne spare, should Tromp 30 abort with platform or sensor problems. In the event all aircraft systems – the two chine-mounted Technical Objective Cameras (TEOCs) for spot coverage and the nose-mounted, Optical Bar Cameras (OBC) for horizon-to-horizon coverage, worked as advertised aboard the primary aircraft and '960 was not called upon to penetrate hostile airspace. Despite SAM launches against '980, the SR-71 proved yet again that it could operate with impunity in such high threat environments, and at 0935 hrs Tromp 30 landed safely back at 'the Hall'. The missions 'take' was processed in the Mobile Processing Centre (MPC), located within one of Mildenhall's disused hangars. It was then transported by a KC-135 (Trout 99) to Andrews AFB, Maryland, where national-level officials were eagerly awaiting post-strike briefings.

Two further missions over Libya were conducted on both 16 and 17 April, with minor route changes and different call signs. This intense period of reconnaissance activity scored many new 'firsts' for Det 4: first occasion that both aircraft were airborne simultaneously; first time KC-10s had been used to refuel SR-71s in the European theatre; first time that photos taken by the SR-71s were released to the press (although the source was never officially admitted and the image quality was purposely, severely degraded to hide true capability). All in all, the missions were a great accomplishment by the Det's

Above and below Just as Senior Crown closed down, Lockheed photographer Eric Schulzinger shot for posterity a masterful series of photographs of the Habu. Here 17968 has had a Dolby X logo applied to its tail. (Eric Schulzinger)

support personnel under the command of ex SR-71 RSO, Lt Col Barry MacKean.

Shutdown

The 'Senior Crown' programme was living on borrowed time without an electro-optical backplate for the camera system and a data-link system which would permit camera imagery and radar data from ASARS-1 to be down-linked in near real time. Eventually, funds were appropriated for the development of Senior King, a secure data link via satellite, but its development would prove too late to save the SR-71.

By the late eighties the list of those articulating an anti SR-71 posture was as long and varied as it was powerful. By 1988 it looked as though the efforts of the antagonists would be successful. But all was not quite lost: Admiral Lee Baggott, Commander in Chief, Atlantic (CINCLANT) required SR-71 coverage of the Kola peninsula as there were no other means of obtaining the quality of coverage required. He took the battle to retain the SR-71 in Europe right to the Joint Chiefs of Staff (JCS) and obtained funding for Det 4 for a further year. Meanwhile, the SR-71 PEM and his action officer were able to secure a commitment from a staffer on the Senate Appropriations Committee for $46 million to keep Kadena and Palmdale open for another year. By now however, it was only a question of time before these valiant rearguard actions faced the inevitable. What was to be the final flight of an SR-71 took place on 6 March 1990, when Ed Yeilding and JT Vida flew '972 on a West-to-East coast record-breaking flight across the United States, before landing at the Smithsonian National Aerospace Museum, Washington DC, where the aircraft was handed over for permanent display. Thereafter, SR-71As ('962, '967 and '968), were placed in storage at Site 2 Palmdale. Two SR-71As ('971 and '980), together with the sole surviving SR-71B ('956) were loaned to NASA, the remaining 13 aircraft (including the hybrid trainer designated SR-71C which consisted of the forward fuselage from a static specimen mated to the wing and rear section of YF-12A, 60-6934), were donated to museums throughout the US. Despite more than forty members of Congress, and many other well placed officials and senior officers voicing their concern over the decision.

During the course of the Gulf War, two requests were made to reactivate the Senior Crown programme, both however were turned down by the same SECDEF who had presided over the aircraft's shutdown - Dick Cheney. That Desert Storm was an overwhelming success for coalition forces is beyond despute; however there were lessons to be learned from the 41-day campaign, not least of which was the lack of timely reconnaissance material available to General Schwarzkopf's field commanders.

It wasn't until March/April 1994 that events in the international arena once more took a turn. Relations

Right, top, middle and bottom SR-71A 17968 is caught on another sortie. The aircraft first flew on 3 August 1966, with Bill Weaver in the front and George Andre in the back; it was retired on 12 February 1990, having accumulated 2,279 flight hours. (Eric Schulzinger)

between North Korea and the United States, at best always strained, reached a new low over the north's refusal to allow inspection of their nuclear sites. At this point Senator Robert Byrd took centre stage. Together with several members of the Armed Services, and various members of Congress, he contended that back in 1990 the Pentagon had consistently lied about the supposed readiness of a replacement for the SR-71. The motivation behind such commitments was not the usual politicking, but one of genuine concern for the maintenance of a platform capable of broad area synoptic coverage.

The campaigning and lobbying paid off as noted in the 'Department of Defence Appropriations Bill 1995', report 103-321, dated July 20, wherein provision was made for a modest, 'three plane SR-71 aircraft contingency reconnaissance capability', at a cost of $100 million, for fiscal year 1995 (FY95). Of the three SR-71As placed in deep storage at Site 2, Palmdale, only '967 was called to arms. The other A model to be recommissioned was '971 which had been loaned to NASA, re-numbered 832 and regularly ground tested but never flown by its civilian caretakers. Pilot trainer SR-71B, together with the brand new flight simulator, would be shared between the Air Force and NASA, and in a further move to keep operating costs to a minimum the new detachment, designated det 2, would,

like NASA, operate its aircraft from Edwards AFB, California.

Aircraft reactivation began on 5 January 1995 and seven days later, at 11:26 hrs, NASA crew Steve Ishmael and Marta Bohn-Meyer got airborne from Edwards in '971 on a 26 minute ferry flight which terminated at Lockheed Martin's Skunk Works, Plant 10 Building 602, Palmdale. Over the next three months ASARS and other sensors previously in storage at Luke AFB, Arizona were installed. At 10:18 hrs on 26 April, NASA crew Ed Schneider and Marta completed a 34 minutes FCF on '971. A month later Ed and Marta's husband Bob Meyer conducted 971's second and final FCF which lasted 2.5 hours. It took seven further FCFs to wring out all the glitches in '967, the final one successfully completed on 12 January 1996.

Three Air Force crews were selected to fly the aircraft, pilots Gil Luloff, Tom McCleary and Don Watkins together with RSOs Blair Bozek, Mike Finan and Jim Greenwood, the plan being that two crews would always be Mission Ready qualified and the third crew, Mission Capable. Whilst crew proficiency training got underway in the simulator and the 'B' model, R&D funds were used to develop and install the long overdue data-link, the antenna for which is housed in a small radome, just

Below Of the two SR-71As loaned to NASA after USAF operations were initially terminated on 22 November 1989, 17971, renumbered NASA 832, was called back to arms and 17967 was pulled from Air Force Site 2, deep storage, Palmdale. (Paul Crickmore)

forward of the front undercarriage wheel well. A digital cassette recorder system (DCRsi) provided recording and playback of both ELINT and ASARS data. Near-real-time data could be provided if the aircraft was within 300n ml line-of-sight range of a receiving station; if not, the entire recorded collection could be downloaded in ten minutes once within station range.

As qualified Air Force crews began to acquaint themselves with their operational aircraft, the long-running battle between the various factions supporting or opposing the resurrected programme came to a head. Exploiting a complex technical loophole in the legislation concerning the deployment of funds which had been assigned by the Senate Appropriations Committee in the FY1996 Defence Appropriations Bill, but not authorised in two other pieces of supporting legislation, it was decided that technically it was illegal to operate the SR-71. Consequently at 23:00 (Z) on 16 April 1996 a signal was despatched from the Pentagon, suspending SR-71 operations with immediate effect. The war between various Senate Committees then escalated, when supporters of the SR-71 program serving on the Senate Appropriations Committee threatened to eliminate section 8080 of the Appropriations Act and defeat the Intelligence Authorization Act for FY97. This would effectively ensure that all intelligence activities for FY97 would grind to a halt - one can imagine the sheer panic this action would have produced in AF, DIA CIA and NSA circles!

Perhaps not surprisingly the tactic worked. Of the $253 billion Defence Budget for 1997, $30 million was allocated for SR-71 Operations & Maintenance and a further $9 million for procurement. This spend was ratified and signed off by President Clinton and the three flight crews once again worked their way up to full proficiency and the ASARS-1 data link worked extremely well. The next major sensor enhancement update involved the development of an electro-optical backplate for the TEOCs by Recon Optical, located in Barrington, Illinois. This would have replaced film and instead enabled high quality, close-look imagery, to be transmitted, also via the data link, in real time, directly to theatre commanders. Unfortunately, political prevarication continued and in October 1997, President Clinton line vetoed the release of further SR-71 funds. On 30 September 1999, the end of the military fiscal year, remaining monies ran out and Senior Crown succumbed. Kelly's prophesy that the SR-71 would prove invulnerable to shoot-downs until at least 2001, failed to take cognisance of the weaponry mustered against the program by various politicians and (self) interest groups within the ranks of his fellow countrymen.

The F-117

During the air war over Vietnam, the most lethal threat facing US air elements was radar directed surface to air missiles (SAMs) and anti-aircraft artillery (AAA). It was extremely disruptive, often resulting in attack aircraft missing their targets in order to evade SAMs or dodge AAA. Latterly, during the 1973 Yom Kippur war, the Israeli Air Force lost 109 aircraft in just eighteen days, virtually all falling victim to radar guided SAM or AAA batteries. With the Soviet Union having developed a highly sophisticated, integrated defence network, US planners estimated that if the Israeli loss ratio were extrapolated into a NATO/War Pact scenario, NATO Air Forces would be decimated in just over two weeks. Clearly, what was needed was a fundamental rethink on how to redress this imbalance.

In 1974, Ken Perko in the Tactical Technology Office (TTO) at the Defence Advanced Research Projects Agency (DARPA), requested submissions from Northrop,

McDonnell Douglas, General Dynamics, Fairchild and Grumman, addressing two considerations:-

1. What were the signature thresholds that an aircraft would need to achieve to become essentially undetectable at an operationally useful range?
2. Did those companies possess the capabilities to design and produce an aircraft with those necessary low signatures?

Fairchild and Grumman declined the invitation to participate, while General Dynamics emphasised the continued need for electronic counter measures. Submissions from McDonnell Douglas and Northrop however demonstrated a grasp of the problem, and consequently, they were awarded contracts worth approximately $100,000 each during the closing months of 1974 to conduct further studies.

On 17 January 1975, 'Kelly' Johnson's protege, Ben Rich, became president of the Skunk Works. It was while Ben was still Kelly's Deputy that the former became aware of the low observability study. Lockheed hadn't been one of the five original companies approached by the DARPA team, simply because it hadn't produced a fighter for nearly ten years (the F-104 starfighter). Ben however, obtained a letter from the CIA, granting the Skunk Works permission to discuss with DARPA the low observable characteristics of the A-12 and D-21 drone. After much negotiating, Lockheed were allowed into the competition without a Government contract – a move that ultimately paid a handsome dividend.

In early 1975, the initial Skunk Works Project Team consisted of Ed Martin (Project Manager), Dick Scherrer and Denys Overholser. Overholser had joined the Skunk Works from Boeing in 1964 and recalls, "When Dick Scherrer asked me, 'How do we shape something to make it invisible to radar?' I said, 'Well, it's simple, you just make it out of flat surfaces, and you tilt those flat surfaces over, sweeping the edges away from the radar view angle, and that way you basically cause the energy to reflect away from the radar, thus limiting the magnitude of the return.'" Such radical thinking had its origins in a discussion Overholser had had with his then boss, Bill Schroeder some years earlier, concerning the mathe-

Top left This early model of Have Blue already depicts several of the type's characteristics: highly facetted, intakes above the wing, inboard cantered tails and highly swept leading edge. (Lockheed Martin)

Left Covered in foil, this wooden model is undergoing RCS tests in Lockheed's anechoic chamber at Rye Canyon. (Lockheed Martin)

Above Phase 1 of the XST programme culminated in RCS evaluations between the two contending designs at the Air Force's Radar Target Scatter (RATSCAT), test range, located at White Sands, New Mexico. (Lockheed Martin)

matics and physics of optical scattering. The two had concluded that detectable signatures could be minimised utilising a shape composed of the smallest number of properly orientated flat panels. In addition, Schroeder believed that it was possible to develop and resolve a mathematical equation capable of calculating the reflection from a triangular flat panel; this in turn he hypothesised could be applied in a calculation relating to RCS. As a result, Overholser hired his ex-boss out of retirement and as Schroeder's mathematical computations became available, Overholser and his team of two engineers were able to use these to write the computer programme that could evaluate the RCS of prospective design submissions nominated by Dick Scherrer and his group of preliminary design engineers. Denys and his team worked night and day and in just five weeks produced an RCS prediction programme known as 'Echo 1'. As tests proceeded, it was determined that the edge contributions calculated by Echo 1 weren't exactly correct, due to a phenomenon known as diffraction. However, shortly after developing Echo 1, Denys became aware of a publication entitled *Method of Edge Waves in the Physical Theory of Diffraction*, published in an unclassified technical paper in the Soviet Union in 1962 by Pyotr Ufimtsev, Chief Scientist at the Moscow Institute of Radio Engineering. The paper had been translated by Air Force Systems Command's Foreign Technology Division in 1971, and Denys was able to incorporate elements of its theory into a refined version of the Echo 1 programme. The resultant model was a facetted delta wing design which drew a healthy share of scepticism from within the Skunk Works, some in aerodynamics referring to the shape as "The Hopeless Diamond". However, with $25,000 procured from the Lockheed board, two, one-third scale, wooden models of the Hopeless Diamond were built, one was used by the aerodynamists, the other to measure RCS values in Lockheed's anechoic chamber. The first series of tests, conducted in June 1975, demonstrated that its RCS 'spikes' matched precisely those predicted by Echo 1. The model was then moved outdoors to a radar test range near Palmdale, in the Mojave Desert. Yet again, test results conformed well with Echo 1 predictions, creating greater levels of confidence in both the computer programme and the facetted design concept.

Lockheed submitted two proposals to DARPA, one included the predicted and measured signature data for the Hopeless Diamond, the other provided the predicted data for an air vehicle of flyable configuration. This came about in response to DARPA issuing proposals to the three competitors for what was to become known as the Experimental Survivable Testbed (XST) programme, which was informally requested in the late summer of 1975.

The Competition

Northrop's XST entry was similar in appearance to that of Lockheed's; its design had been developed from a computer programme called GENSCAT. This also had its origins in mathematical equations associated with the physics of optics. McDonnell Douglas had been the first to determine what the RCS thresholds for the competition were likely to be, however they were unable to design an aircraft that could achieve anything like those

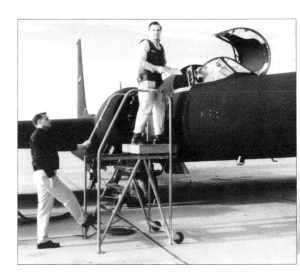

goals. With RCS results from both Lockheed and Northrop verging on the revolutionary, DARPA determined that the program should be developed into a two-phase, full-scale, flight test demonstration. Phase 1 would culminate in a ground RCS evaluation of large scale models, following which one contractor would be selected to proceed with phase two: the construction and flight testing of two demonstration vehicles. The estimated cost for the XST programme was $36,000,000 and this would be split between the successful contractor, the Air Force and DARPA. On 1 November 1975, Lockheed and Northrop were each awarded contracts of $1.5 million to conduct phase one of the XST programme.

In early April 1976, Lockheed received word that they had officially won that phase of the competition. However the outstanding results also achieved by the Northrop team caused DARPA to urge them to remain together. Shortly thereafter Northrop successfully submitted studies for a Battlefield Surveillance Aircraft, Experimental (BSAX) which became Tacit Blue - the highly successful flight demonstration programme that provided vital data for the subsequent B-2 bomber program.

Phase two of the XST programme was code-named Have Blue, and was initiated on 26 April 1976, when the Skunk Works were authorised to proceed with the design, construction and flight testing of two technology demonstrator aircraft.

Have Blue had three objectives:

1. Validate, in flight, the four low observability signatures identified earlier in the programme, (radar, infrared, acoustic and visual).
2. Demonstrate acceptable performance and flying qualities.
3. Demonstrate modelling capabilities that accurately predict low observable characteristics of an aircraft in flight.

Manufacturing was placed under the direction of Bob Murphy and the entire Engineering, Fabrication and Assembly of Have Blue was carried out in legendary Building 82 (birthplace of the F-104, U-2 and A-12).

Just three assembly tools were used on the project; wing, forward fuselage and aft fuselage. The sub assemblies were all made on a tooling plate left over from where the main frames for the C-5 Galaxy had been machined. On the morning of Wednesday 16 November the prototype Have Blue (HB1001) was flown by C-5 from Burbank to Area 51, where it was reassembled and readied for a final series of pre-flight tests. On 1 December 1977, Bill Park completed HB1001's maiden flight.

The first five sorties in aircraft number one were completed by Bill, who was chased on each occasion by Air Force Test Pilot Ken Dyson in a T-38. On 17 January 1978, Ken completed his first flight in the Have Blue prototype. All was proceeding well and on 4 May 1978, Bill had conducted 24 flights on HB1001 and Ken, twelve. However, whilst returning to Area 51 that day, Bill was involved in a landing incident which damaged one of the aircraft's main undercarriage legs. Retracting the gear and going-around for another landing attempt Bill discovered that the damaged leg would only half extend. Despite several attempts to free the jam by pounding the other main wheel on the runway, it steadfastly refused to budge. As fuel depleted, the decision was made to climb the aircraft to 10,000ft and for Bill to eject. However, on the climb, the aircraft ran out of gas and Bill was forced to eject, during the course of which he hit his head and was knocked out. Still unconscious when he hit the ground, he sustained back and leg injuries that forced an early retirement from test flying.

It would take a further six months to prepare HB1002 for its maiden flight; an event which took place early on the morning of the 20 July 1978. Ken Dyson recalls, "We

Above left Lockheed chief test pilot, Bill Park (in flight suit), was first to fly the Have Blue prototype HB1001. (Lockheed Martin)

Above Maj Norman 'Ken' Dyson was recruited into the Have Blue program whilst serving as Director of the F-15 Joint Test Force. (Lockheed Martin)

Below HB1001 received this ingenious three colour-three tone camouflage pattern to hide the facetting from uncleared 'onlookers'. (Lockheed Martin)

flew three flights to check the aeroplane out, then on 9 August 1978, we began to take the first airborne RCS measurements. I flew against a ground based facility and on these first series of tests, they wanted to check-out the cross-section of the aeroplane nose-on, that's with a look angle of zero. To achieve this, I climbed to a predetermined altitude and maintained a heading that would take me right over the radar test site. When I reached the test point, I configured the aeroplane in a decent, making sure my speed, angle of attack and rate of decent was exactly correct. I had to keep control movements to a minimum in order to provide accurate test data, so I switched in the autopilot. Well, as soon as I did that, the nose went right and the wing rolled slightly left. I later learned that Ben Rich, who was watching the test in the radar control room went crazy, asking, 'What does that goddamn Air Force pilot think he is doing! Is he deliberately side-slipping the aeroplane to screw-up our test results?' I decided to switch-off the autopilot and fly manually, something we'd planned not to do, because the test engineers didn't think the necessary tight parameters could be achieved manually. Well it seemed to work pretty good, and after that, I flew all the tests manually - we never did resolve the problem with the autopilot. Virtually every flight in aeroplane two was associated with RCS measurements and if we weren't measuring radar returns, we would be flying the aeroplane against operational systems to see if they could see us. To my knowledge, none did."

On 29 June 1979, Dyson air aborted HB1002 shortly after take off, following a fluctuating hydraulic pressure reading. He continues, "On 10 July, we flew again and the aeroplane was OK. The next day I got airborne and had the chase aeroplane look me over, everything was OK, so I flew outbound to get to a point to run against an F-15 Eagle, to see how it performed against us. I was

Above HB1002 was the RCS test vehicle and was flown throughout its life by Ken Dyson. Its external appearance differed from the prototype; gone is the instrumented nose-boom and the drag 'chute receptacle. (Lockheed Martin)

Below HB1002 accumulated 52 test sorties before being lost on 20 July 1978. (Lockheed Martin)

just short of the designated turn point, when I noticed the same hydraulic system begin to oscillate, again in the downward direction. I thought well, that's the end of this flight and turned back. I started to tell test control about my problem, when I got a fire light. After pulling the power back, and telling them of my troubles, I shut the engine down. All this was in short order. I had the aeroplane pointed towards home plate and configured at the right speed for single engine operation (it was not a good performer on a single engine, not much thrust, and a lot of drag). I was coming home somewhere between 20 and 25,000 ft. Shortly after that, the remaining hydraulic system began to oscillate in a downward direction and I knew that was not good for our unstable machine. Just about the time the remaining hydraulic system went to zero, the plane pitched violently down, something like 7 negative 'g's, it then pitched up, the pitch rates were just eye watering, something only an unstable machine could do. I was somewhere around 225 knots and above 20,000ft and the aeroplane was tossing me up and down and actually got near vertical nose down and near vertical nose up. I began to try and reach for the ejection seat ring that was between my legs. I got my hand on it and pulled. The canopy blew off, the seat went out and I found myself floating under a 'chute at about 20,000 ft."

As Ken slowly descended by 'chute, the pilot of the F-15 with whom he had planned to conduct further tests began orbiting above. Col Norm Suits, the Director of the F-15 Joint Test Force, saw the stricken Have Blue aircraft impact the ground and shortly afterwards, spotted two unauthorised cross country vehicles heading towards the crash site. Although the vehicle's occupants were probably intent on performing their public duty and offering help and assistance to any survivors, the highly classified nature of the program and the materials used in its design couldn't be compromised. Acting on his own

Above Despite initial skepticism over the 'Hopeless Diamond' concept, Dick Cantrell and his team of aerodynamicists worked tirelessly to ensure that the F-117 retained the smallest RCS and remained aerodynamically viable. (Lockheed Martin)

Below As president of the Lockheed Martin Skunk Works, Ben Rich was the driver behind the stealth concept; he passed away on 5 January 1995. (Lockheed Martin)

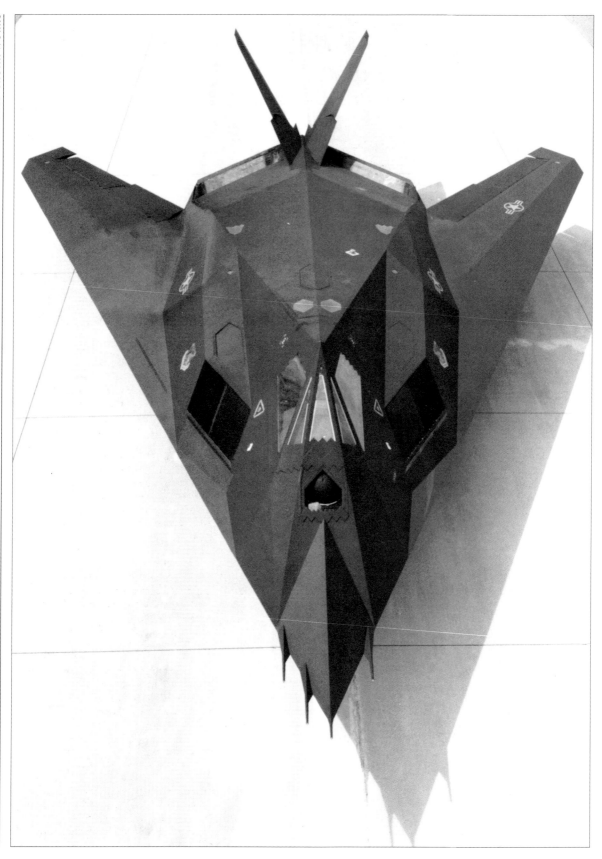

Below Although ice encrustation was not an issue on the Have Blue research vehicles, much time, thought and effort was devoted to the problem on the F-117, before this simple wiper blade was developed. (Paul Crickmore)

Left The F-117 is at its most stealthy head-on, 25 degrees look-down and 25 degrees look-up. Note suck-in doors located above the intakes to supplement air flow at low engine operating speeds. (Lockheed Martin)

initiative, Norm began a series of extremely low passes at the vehicles to deter their drivers from closing in on the wreckage. Just how low these passes were, can only be judged from the fact that he succeeded in his objective!

Ken continues, "I had noted my take off time, and while hanging in my 'chute I noted that ten minutes had elapsed from take-off. I watched the unstable machine flip flop slowly it seemed, as it descended vertically below me and I saw it hit the ground and erupt into a ball of fire, it still had a lot of gas on board. It took me quite a while to make my parachute descent down to the desert floor, after landing (that was my first and only jump to date), I again noted the time, I had been in the parachute for ten minutes".

The cause of the crash was determined to be an engine exhaust clamp, which had become loose, allowing hot exhaust gases to enter the right engine compartment. This had triggered the fire warning light, and as the temperature built up, first the left and then the right hydraulic lines failed, which in turn caused a complete loss of control.

Fortunately the program was within two or three sorties of its planned completion, which officially ended in December 1979. Having achieved all its test objectives, the Have Blue programme can be categorised as a stunning success.

Senior Trend

In June 1977 the Air Force set up a special project office in the Pentagon; its objective, to exploit low observable technology then being demonstrated in phase one of the XST program, and in addition, to initiate conceptual studies into a manned strike aircraft program, referred to as the Advanced Technology Aircraft (ATA) program. Two sets of preliminary requirements for the ATA were developed: ATA 'A', a single seat attack aircraft, with a 5,000 lb payload and 400 n mile range; and ATA 'B', a two-seat bomber with a 10,000 lb payload and 1,000 n mile range.

An $11.1 million concept definition contract was awarded to the Skunk Works on 10 October 1977, for a one year study, based on these two sets of requirements.

As assimilation of the two proposals continued, it became increasingly apparent that ATA 'B' (despite being strongly favoured by Strategic Air Command, following cancellation by the Carter administration of the B-1A), was in the upper right corner of what was at that time considered realistically achievable.

Consequently in the summer of 1978, Air Force officials decided to terminate further studies involving ATA 'B' and instead, opted to proceed with ATA 'A' into full scale development (FSD).

Covert funds were established, and key individuals serving on various government committees were briefed on the programme. On 1 November 1978, production was authorised, the programme accorded the code name 'Senior Trend' and Lockheed were awarded a $340 million contract to cover the cost of building five full-scale development aircraft, plus, provide spares, support and flight testing (this amount did not include the cost of purchasing the aircraft's General Electric engines).

The production timescales for this revolutionary aircraft program were tight; its first flight was planned for July 1980 - hence the last three digits of the prototype's serial number, 780. Initial Operational Capability (IOC) was to be achieved in March 1982, with a planned production run of twenty aircraft. Construction of FSD1, the prototype F-117A, (Aircraft 780) commenced at Burbank in November 1979.

Technical Specifications

The F-117A Nighthawk is a survivable interdictor; the determinant in achieving this goal has been the development of Very Low Observable (VLO) techniques. To confound the principal detection medium - radar - design focused upon producing a low radar cross section (RCS). The reduction of an aircraft's RCS to levels that would provide an explicit operational advantage had been the 'holy grail' for many military aircraft designers since the latter stages of World War Two.

Over subsequent years, development work had, by and large, been focused on producing materials capable of absorbing incident radiation to varying degrees. Although the use of Radar Absorbing Materials (RAM) certainly achieved a reduction in RCS, this was not enough to gain 'an explicit operational advantage'; that could only be achieved when designers were able to build a shape both capable of performing an operational mission and producing an RCS lower by several orders of magnitude than any current conventional aircraft. It was here that the odds were definitely stacked against the designers, as perfectly demonstrated by the radar equation which basically states that, 'detection range is proportional to the fourth root of the radar cross section'. That is to say, in order to reduce detection range by a factor of ten, it is necessary to reduce the target aircraft's RCS by a factor of 10,000, or 40 dBs.

Having established the required RCS signature levels from various look angles, together with the overall shape required to meet those goals, it then becomes necessary to consider other aspects of the aircraft's design that will impact on RCS values. For a conventional jet aircraft, these include the air-intake and exhaust cavities, the aircraft's cockpit, etc. Thus to prevent radar energy

Above All sixty F-117As were constructed within the Skunk Works facilities at Burbank. (Lockheed Martin)

Below The F-117 is powered by two General Electric F404-GE-F1D2 engines. (Lockheed Martin)

reflecting back from numerous corner reflectors inside the cockpit, the F-117A's cockpit windows are metallised, much like metallised sunglasses; allowing the pilot to see out, but to all other intents, performing as a facetted panel in relation to electromagnetic radiation, reflecting energy away from its source.

The RAM coating applied over the rest of the aircraft was originally made up of 8 feet by 2 feet sheets (designated BX210), which were glued onto the aircraft's surface like linoleum tiles. The process was extremely time consuming and expensive, costing $750,000 dollars just in labour to apply the material. As a result, a computer controlled spray coating was developed, which is environmentally safe, bonds satisfactorily to the aircraft and preserves the required radar attenuation characteristics. The original compound was known as BX199, but its durability and maintainability was improved upon and it evolved

In addition to producing a low RCS, the F-117A designers also paid good attention to reducing electromagnetic emissions and infrared radiation from the aircraft's hot parts. An important feature regarding design for low observability is that in general, the design of an aircraft does not have to be compromised to negate the different 'observables'. For example, if something is good for reducing radar returns, it can generally be made good for reducing infrared returns and vice versa. It was therefore appropriate to shield the exhaust nozzle for both radar and infrared reasons.

Range specifications of ATA 'A' dictated planning for the aircraft to be in theatre, which immediately identified the principal radar types to be deceived in order to significantly enhance survivability. These were airborne intercept and SAM radars, which typically operate on a wave length of between 3 and 10 centimetres. It was soon determined that flying at supersonic speed didn't enhance survivability. Indeed, flying at high subsonic speeds actu-

Above Taken during a training sortie in the flight simulator, the cockpit layout is pre-OCIP phase 3. (Lockheed Martin)

Below The current, post-OCIP phase 3 cockpit includes an active liquid crystal display, incorporated in the Heads-Up Display (HUD). (Lockheed Martin)

ally increased survivability by reducing a defender's ability of detecting and tracking the aircraft using infrared
systems. It was therefore decided that the platform would
be powered by non afterburning engines, which also
reduced airframe temperatures, further lowering its IR
signature.

Optimum weapon effectiveness was achieved by placing
the aircraft at medium altitude, which, for a subsonic
aircraft, touting a modest performance envelope, would be
utter suicide - were it not for stealth. The aspect which
presents a defender with the greatest chance of a successful intercept is the frontal zone. If the threshold of
detection, by radars using wavelengths of between 3 and
10 cm, can be foiled to a point where the aircraft is just
one minute flying time (about ten miles), from the radar
head, then there is a good chance of avoiding a successful
intercept. Pulling all the strands together therefore, an F-
117A, flying at an altitude of 12,000 feet and 500 knots,
will achieve that one minute detection goal parameter by
being at its most 'stealthy', head on, 25 degrees look
down, and 25 degrees look up.

Powered by two General Electric F404-GE F1D2 two
shaft, low-bypass-ratio turbofans the F-117A Nighthawk

Right Target acquisition is achieved using this Forward Looking
Infra red (FLIR) turret. As the 'look-angle' increases, the target
is 'handed-off' to the Downward Looking Infra red (DLIR)
turret, located within the aircraft's underside, for final target
tracking. Together, the two units are referred to as the Infrared
Acquisition and Detection System (IRADS). (Paul Crickmore)

Below The F-117 is capable of hauling a wide variety of hard-
ware, including the B61 nuclear weapon. (Lockheed Martin)

has a maximum sea level thrust rating of 10,800lbs. The engine gearbox drives the main fuel pump, the oil pump assembly, the engine alternator and the PTO shaft, which powers the Airframe Mounted Accessory Drive (AMAD). Total fuel capacity is approximately 19,000 lbs or 2,800 US gallons of JP-8.

Senior Trend's original avionics package was based around three Delco M362 F computers with 32k words of 16 bit core memory, as used in the F-16. However, in 1984, its avionics architecture was the subject of a three phase Offensive Capability Improvement Program (OCIP). Phase 1, the Weapon System Computational Subsystem (WSCS) upgrade program was initiated to replace the Delco M362F's with IBM AP-102 MIL-STD-1750A computers. These new units boosted the capability of 1 million instructions per second, 16 bit CPU with 128k words of 16 bit memory expandable to 256k.

Phase II of OCIP, afforded greater situational awareness, and reduced pilot workload, by allowing a 4D Flight Management System to fly complex profiles automatically, providing speed and time over target (TOT) control. Also included in this phase was the installation of Colour Multi functional Display Indicators and a Digital Tactical Situation Display or moving map; a new Data Entry Panel, a Display Processor, an Auto Throttle System and a Pilot Activated Automatic Recovery System (PAARS).

OCIP phase III saw the replacement of the ageing SPN-GEANS, INS system, with a new Honeywell H-423/E Ring Laser Gyro (RLG). The original acronym for this programme was to have been RNIP, which stands for Ring Laser Gryro, Navigation Improvement Programme. However, the system was supplemented with a Rockwell-Collins Global Positioning System (GPS) thereby giving rise to the title RNIP plus. The new INS vastly reduces alignment time from 43 minutes for SPN-GEANS, to just 9 minutes and considerably enhances overall reliability, increasing the mean time between failure from 400 to 2,000 hours. In itself, the H-423 may not boost enhanced accuracy (still believed to be 0.12 n m/h), however, when used in association with GPS, the system represents a significant advance in navigational accuracy.

Flight Testing

In 1977, Lt Col Dave Ferguson commanded the 6513th Test Squadron, a unit which had its administrative headquarters together with a small number of F-4s and T-38s at Edwards Air Force Base. However, the 6513th had a black side, seven of its other aircraft were involved in a highly classified programme known as 'Red Hat', these aircraft were MiG-17s and MiG-21s based up at Area 51. It was whilst carrying out his duties at 'a remote test site', that Dave met Bill Park. At that time, Bill was the Director of Flight Operations for the Skunk Works, but he hadn't flown military jets since his involvement in Project Tagboard, the M-21/D-21 drone evaluations that had taken place nearly ten years earlier. Bill was gearing up to fly Have Blue and Dave was asked to get him re-qualified. This was achieved in a T-38 and through this initial contact, Dave flew the occasional T-38 chase sortie during the Have Blue programme. In 1978, Bill offered Dave a job on the Senior Trend Programme, which he accepted following his retirement from the Air Force in 1979. Earlier that same year Bill Park hired Harold 'Hal'

Below Having been delivered by C-5 Galaxy from Burbank to Area 51, the F-117A prototype (FSD1) is undergoing final assembly. (Lockheed Martin)

Above The prototype's serial - 780 - would prove to represent an over-optimistic first flight target date, with FSD1 completing that task on 18 June 1981. (Lockheed Martin)

Farley in as the projects chief pilot, having poached him from Grumman. Tom Morgenfeld became the third pilot recruited, having worked prior with the YF-18 project development team.

In addition to contractor pilots, it had been decided that developmental together with category I and II, operational test and evaluation (OT&E) of the F-117A, would be conducted by a Joint Test Force. Tactical Air Command (TAC), controlled testing and initially provided three pilots and two analysts. The third party involved in this 'tripartite' force, was Air Force Systems Command. They provided three pilots, four engineers and approximately forty aircraft maintenance personnel.

To prepare themselves for the first series of flights in the F-117A, the team contacted Calspan, and asked them to provide a flight simulation programme based on aerodynamic data acquired through wind tunnel tests and Have Blue. As the programme was so highly classified, the data was delivered to Rogers Smith of Calspan by Hal, Dave, Tom and Bob Loschke, in a restaurant out at Newhall. During that meeting they detailed their requirements from Calspan, without telling Smith what he would be simulating; all he had to work from was a set of aerodynamic data of the predicted flight characteristics of the aircraft in the landing pattern. Rogers Smith took the information with him to Buffalo, New York, to create a simulation which would be programmed into the Lockheed/Calspan NT-33A.

This aircraft enabled the predicted stability and control aspects of different aircraft to be simulated, allowing pilots to familiarise themselves with the likely characteristics to be encountered prior to their first real flights. In keeping with earlier Skunk Works, blackworld, aircraft development projects, flight testing would be conducted at the now legendary Area 51. On 1 January 1979,

Below Chief test pilot Hal Farley, prepares to vacate the cockpit upon successfully completing the F-117's first flight. (Lockheed Martin)

preparations at the remote site got underway to receive the latest guest.

Back at Burbank, the first production engine arrived in April 1980 and on 2 September, the first engine run was conducted. The complex design and engineering of the exhaust nozzle caused more than a few headaches and on 22 December, the team suffered the first of several nozzle failures. This led to further delays with to first flight. However, on 12 February 1981, an improved nozzle was fitted, which helped to eradicate at least some of the problems.

On 16 January 1981, a C-5 from Burbank touched down at Groom Lake, onboard was Aircraft 780, FSD 1 - the combined test team at last had an aircraft. It wasn't until 18 June 1981 that Hal Farley was finally able to

take Aircraft 780 on its first flight, an event cut short due, yet again, to a temperature build-up in the exhaust section. However, the significance of this event was such that film footage shot during the sortie was edited at the test area into a one-minute sequence. It was then flown by special courier aircraft to Andrews AFB, and then taken to the White House, where it was viewed by President Reagan.

The second FSD aircraft, '781, was flown for the first time by Dave Ferguson, on 24 September 1981. After completing just four sorties however, it underwent considerable rework, which included retro fitting larger interim tail units and a 'production' nose section, which, after further tests, housed the Infrared Acquisition and Designation System (IRADS) units. In addition, an asymmetric, four-probe, production configured air data system was added.

It was decided to qualify the aircraft for air refuelling (A/R), early in the programme; the first such sortie being flown by AFSC test pilot Skip Anderson, on 17 November 1981. Once A/R qualified, the test program further accelerated, as evidenced by a flight completed by Hal in '780, just two days later, which lasted 2.8hrs. The first night flight of an F-117A was completed by Roger Moseley flying Aircraft '782 on the 22 March 1982; he flew the same aircraft on the 19 April 1982, successfully conducting the first night air refuelling.

Low Observability airborne testing of the F-117A was exhaustive. For '783's fourth flight, TAC pilot Tom Abel went airborne on 15 July 1982 to conduct IR tests of Senior Trend with the help on an NKC-135, an exercise repeated the next day by Pete Barnes. Four flights were then flown against an F-4 to evaluate the IR threat from air-launched heat seeking missiles. By 13 January 1983, Air Force pilots had flown '783 on no less than 21 RCS

Above After ten flights, FSD1 was grounded for over ten months, while larger tail units were fitted to improve directional stability. The earlier desert-camouflage paint pattern was also removed and replaced by an overall, low-visibility grey scheme. (Lockheed Martin)

Below For a month FSD1 had wing leading edge extensions added during an evaluation of its handling qualities. (Lockheed Martin)

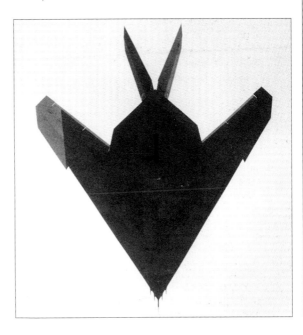

and IR sorties. These included cued and uncued tests against the best US detection systems available, in addition to 'Special Category' tests, flown against Soviet-made equipment 'acquired' through various means by the United States. One particular test, flown by John Beesley on 3 December 1982, included taking RCS measurements while the aircraft's right bomb-bay door was open - a period when the aircraft is at its most vulnerable.

Aircraft '783 continued to be the 'fleet's' RCS work-horse throughout 1984, with analysis of the air-air threat continuing. On 24 April, an F-16 made four radar passes against the aircraft, two days later, thirteen radar passes were made by the Fighting Falcon.

By late July, F-15s, F-14s and an EF-111 had conducted similar threat tests against '783. Thereafter, it was utilised alternately between low observability tests and evaluations, and the integration of improvements made to the navigation and weapons delivery systems.

Aircraft '784, FSD 5, was the dedicated IRADS test and evaluation ship, consequently its first 106 flights were made in pursuit of this task; after which on 23 September 1983, it was placed in temporary storage.

At the end of November 1984, the aircraft was dismantled and moved, via C-5, from Area 51 back to Burbank. The operational limitations of an infrared targeting

Right and below Having qualified the F-117 for air refuelling from a KC-135 on 17 November 1981, Senior Trend was cleared to tank from KC-10 Extenders on 8 September 1983. (Lockheed Martin)

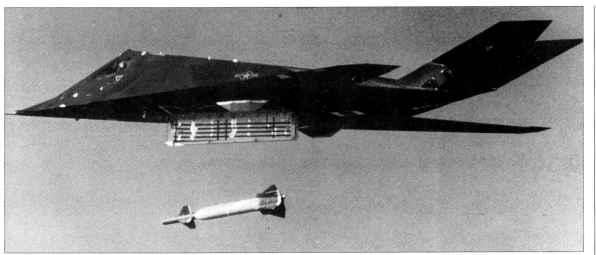

Above FSD5, serial '784, the final developmental aircraft, completed its first flight on 10 April 1982. It is seen here dropping a 2,000lb GBU-27 practice bomb during separation trials. (Lockheed Martin)

Left Initially equipped with the GBU-10, the Paveway II guidance unit corrected the weapons trajectory using full deflection commands to the canards. This had a negative impact on the weapon's performance. (Lockheed Martin)

Below The GBU-27 featured an improved Paveway III guidance section and when dropped for the first time by Jim Dunn, from '783, the inert weapon scored a direct hit on the 55 gallon barrel target, splitting it in half! (Lockheed Martin)

system with which to aim weapons (however accurately), was already fully appreciated. Consequently, Aircraft 784 underwent modifications to install a low observable radar system to conduct both ground mapping and target acquisition.

It was returned to Area 51 and from September 1985, until the end of the year 34 sorties totalling 45.5hrs were flown, during which time all aspects of the radar mapping and targeting system in '784 were evaluated: RCS of the antenna and radome; the ability of the system to perform the ground mapping task; threat evaluation during system

operation; system resolution including four sorties which were flown by 4450th TFG pilot, Maj William Aten (Bandit 164), enabling the system to be evaluated from a front line pilot's perspective. Those involved in this evaluation have stated that the system was remarkable and incredibly stealthy.

However, it was not deployed operationally for reasons of cost and on the basis that, to date, Senior Trend as a concept, had not been tested under actual combat conditions, something of a Catch 22 - stealth still had its 'doubting Thomases'.

After a three year programme to improve the aircraft's RAM coating, a compound known as BX185 was developed. A one-quarter scale model is seen being made ready for RCS evaluations at Lockheed's Helendale test range. (Lockheed Martin)

When the test detachment at Area 51 changed command on 14 December 1983, John Beesley completed a fly-by in '782 patriotically adorned. (USAF)

Tonopah

Formed on 15 October 1979, designated the 4450th Tactical Group, and referred to as A-unit, the Air Force's first operational F-117 unit was commanded by Col Robert "Burner" Jackson and would be located at the Tonopah Test Range, located northwest of Nellis AFB, Nevada. A security cover story for the blackworld unit was provided by twenty Ling Tempo Vaught A-7Ds and a small number of two seat A-7Ks. These were based at Nellis AFB and referred to as P-Unit. The 4450th Test Squadron (established on the 11 June 1981), was referred to as I-Unit and Detachment 1 of A-Unit, based at Tonopah, was Q-Unit. In addition to providing the 'avionics testing' cover story, the A-7s were used to maintain pilot proficiency until F-117As became available and were also used as chase aircraft.

Supplemental to overseeing the construction program, Col Bob Jackson also set about recruiting the initial cadre of pilots, as Al Whitley, at that time a Major, recalls: "My interview occurred in late 1980 at the Nellis AFB, Visiting Officers Quarters. When the time came for the interview, I proceeded to the designated meeting place - Colonel Jackson's room. When I knocked on the door, it opened slightly and Colonel Jackson asked to see my identification card. I produced it, the door closed, and a few seconds later he opened the door and said 'Yes, you're Whitley, come in'. In the next few minutes, Colonel Jackson told me very little about a program which would involve significant family separation, yet the opportunity to not only remain at Nellis AFB for another full assignment, but also the chance to fly the A-7 again. He didn't say much more, other than I would have no opportunity to discuss it with my wife and that I had five minutes to make up my mind. With no hesitation, I said, 'Sign me up'. Colonel Jackson said he'd be contacting me in the future on specifics. That was the end of the interview." In the spring of 1981, Lt Colonel Jerry Fleming the Squadron Commander called Whitley and a couple of the new members of the unit to a remote, secure location in Area ll (or Lake Mead Base) of the Nellis AFB complex. There, for the first time, they were shown photos of what they would be flying. Whitley remembers: "I was genuinely excited and honoured to be part of something that was on the 'leading edge' of technology.

I quickly added a new word to my vocabulary that would have a significant impact on the rest of my Air Force career – 'stealth'."

The original plan was that the unit should achieve initial operational capability (IOC), forty months after aircraft '780's first flight, which was scheduled for July 1980. Therefore Q-Unit, nicknamed the 'Goatsuckers', were expected to assume a limited operational role in November 1982. This was not achieved owing to various design and manufacturing obstacles. In fact, the first production aircraft, number '785, didn't attempt its first flight until 20 April 1982. As with the previous FSD aircraft, aeroplane number one, from Lot 2, had been completed at Burbank and flown via C-5 Galaxy to Area 51. There it had been re-assembled and following various ground checks, Lockheed test pilot Bob Riendenauer

In March 1991, the combined test force put this formation together; it depicts '781, '782, '783 and '831. '780 had already been retired. (Lockheed Martin)

The first home for F-117 operations was Tonopah. Note the 'drive-through' barns, grouped in blocks of six. (Lockheed Martin)

advanced the throttles and began his take-off run. The aircraft rotated as planned, but immediately after lift off everything went horribly wrong. The nose yawed violently, it then pitched up and completed a snap roll which left it on its back before impacting the ground. It was nothing short of a miracle that Bob survived, not so though aircraft '785, which was totally wrecked. A post accident investigation established that the pitch and yaw rate gyro input to the flight control computer had been cross wired.

In September, detachment 1 of the 4450th was designated the 4452nd Test Squadron and it was while the unit had a complement of just two aircraft that another milestone was achieved. On the night of Friday

15 October, Major Al Whitley conducted his first Senior Trend flight and in so doing, also became the first operational pilot to fly the aircraft.

The sporadic nature of the delivery schedule continued and by the end of 1982, the unit still only boasted seven aircraft. Col James S. Allen had assumed command of the 4450th, from Col Bob Jackson on 17 May 1982 and by 28 October 1983, Senior Trend was deemed to have achieved Limited Initial Operational Capability (LIOC). As the potential of Senior Trend became increasingly more apparent to those cleared into the program, the procurement plan was increased to a total of 57 aircraft (the final total was 59). The impact of this decision created the need for two additional squadrons, consequently in July 1983, I-Unit "Nightstalkers", was activated, to be followed in October 1985 by Z-Unit , "Grim Reapers" (later redesignated the 4450th Test Squadron and the 4453rd Test and Evaluation Squadron respectively).

Aircraft Losses

Unlike their Senior Trend counterparts at Area 51, the operational pilots at TTR lived a bat-like existence, - sleeping during the day and flying only at night, it was both highly demanding and chronically tiring. At 01:13 hours on Friday 11 July 1986, in excellent weather and good visibility, Maj Ross E Mulhare departed Tonopah in aircraft '792, callsign Ariel 31. 31 minutes later, '792 ploughed into a hillside 2,280 ft above sea level, killing its

---

Above A-7s were used to provide pilots with a cover story for the 4450th's actual mission. (USAF)

Below Pilots of the 37th TFW, 416 TFS (Ghost Riders), attend a training briefing. (USAF)

Above Ordinance specialists load a 2,000lb GBU-10 practice bomb aboard a 37 TFW aircraft (USAF).

Right In April 1986, two RAF test pilots from Boscombe Down were invited to evaluate the F-117 at Tonopah, a fact that remained shrouded in secrecy for over ten years. One of them, Sqd Ldr Dave Southwood, is seen pictured in an ETPS Jaguar. (Crown Copy DERA, Boscombe Down)

pilot. The prime reason behind this horrific accident was almost certainly pilot fatigue and spatial disorientation.

The 4450th lost a second F-117A and pilot on 14 October 1987. Major Michael C Stewart got airborne from Tonopah at 19:53 hours, in aircraft '815, callsign BURNR 54. In common with the loss of '792, the accident report failed to clearly determine the cause, but yet again, repeated references were made to pilot fatigue and disorientation.

Six days after the tragic loss of Major Stewart, the 4450th became the centre of more unwanted attention, prompted by the loss of yet another of its aircraft. On this occasion Major Bruce L Teagarden (Bandit 222) safely ejected from an A-7D after the aircraft lost power. Disastrously, the A-7 crashed into the Ramada Inn Hotel, near Indianapolis airport, killing nine people in the process. Following a detailed accident investigation however, Bruce was cleared of all culpability surrounding

Above On 10 November 1988, moves began to ease Senior Trend out of the Black, when Assistant Secretary of Defence J Daniel Howard first showed off this grainy picture at a Pentagon press conference. (USAF)

Below In September 1989, the 37th traded in its A-7s for more fuel efficient T-38s. (Lockheed Martin)

Above F-117A 802, first flew on 7 March 1984, it is pictured here over Lake Tahoe. (Lockheed Martin)

the tragic incident. Although publicly acknowledged as being a member of the 4450th, the unit was not known to have any links with Tonopah, ensuring that Senior Trend remained in the black.

During a Pentagon press conference on 10 November 1988, Assistant Secretary of Defense J. Daniel Howard, revealed to the world an extremely 'grainy' photograph of the F-117 and Senior Trend was slowly eased into the 'white world'.

Gone was the need to shelter the 4450th's covert activity behind a valid aircraft type. Consequently in September 1989, the Wing said farewell to the trusty 'Sluff' and instead operated far more economical T-38A Talons, and later AT-38Bs, in the chase pilot proficiency role. Yet another change took place on 5 October 1989: the 4450th TG, together with its component squadrons, was redesignated. The parent designation was changed to the 37th Tactical Fighter Wing, the 4450th (Nightstalkers) together with the 4451st Test Squadron, became the 415th (Nightstalkers) and the 416th (Ghost Riders) respectively. The 4453rd Test and Evaluation Squadron (Grim

Reapers) continued in its responsibility as the Wings training squadron, becoming instead the 417th Tactical Fighter Training Squadron (Bandits). The new designations had a proud historical provenance, being the first US night-fighter squadrons of the Second World War.

Just Cause

The F-117A received its baptism of fire on the night of 19/20 December 1989, whilst participating in a highly controversial action against General Noriega of Panama, codenamed Operation Just Cause. Panama had no defensive radar network. However, it was decided to commit these high value assets on the basis of their bombing accuracy. Consequently, eight F-117s from the 415th TFS took off from Tonopah. Two aircraft were airborne spares and returned to Tonopah following completion of the

Below The USAF took delivery of its last F-117A, aircraft '843 on 12 July 1990. (Lockheed Martin)

initial AR, two aircraft in the lead cell, were targeted to attack an army base at Rio Hato, 65 miles southwest of Panama city. The four remaining aircraft were to take part in an operation which remains classified, but involved special forces attempting to capture Noriega. This element of the mission was air aborted through lack of ground intelligence. The three thousand mile round trip required five AR's, and was supported by KC-10s from the 22nd Air Refuelling Wing, out of March AFB. This ever dependable unit, actually escorted the F-117As from Tonopah, all the way down to the Panamanian coast and back! The objective of Major Greg Feest, flying lead, in aircraft '816, and his wingman Major Dale Hanner (Bandit 239) was to drop one weapon apiece, in an open field adjacent to barracks belonging to Battalion 2000, a unit known to be loyal to Noriega. Their purpose was to stun the sleeping soldiers and disorientate them before they had an opportunity to engage parachute landings by the 2nd and elements of the 3rd Ranger Battalion. However, three hours before the invasion was due to begin, the PDF were alerted to the impending attack and deployed to one of the Ranger's objectives - an air strip. As the two F-117As approached their target area, the wind changed direction, a target change was called, causing confusion; the subsequent bombing results were at best questionable. The Chairman of the House Armed Services Committee, Les Aspin, later stated that target acquisition problems had also added to the pilots' confusion because, "The humid, varied, vegetation... lowered the contrast and gave the [IRAD] system problems".

Desert Storm

At about 2am (Baghdad time) on 1/2 August 1990, three Iraqi Republican Guard divisions invaded Kuwait. In just four days Iraq secured the annexation of Kuwait and were massed menacingly along the Kuwaiti-Saudi border. A further push into Saudi Arabia would not only establish Iraq as the secular leader of the Arab world, but would result in their controlling 45% of the world's oil.

Within two days, F-15C Eagles, KC-10 tankers, E-3 AWACS and C-5 Galaxy transporters - carrying advanced elements of the 82nd Airborne Division - had arrived in Saudi Arabia to draw "a line in the sand", Operation Desert Shield had begun.

On 19 August 1990, 22 F-117s from the 415 TFS staged through Langley AFB en route to King Khalid Air Base, Saudi Arabia. (USAF)

Eighteen F-117s from the 415 TFS, led by Lt Col Greg Feest arrived at King Khalid AB, at around noon, local time on Tuesday 21 August. Soon nicknamed Tonopah East, the facilities offered at the airbase were second to none and lay well beyond the range of Iraqi Scud-B missiles; however, on the down side, the return distance from the base to Baghdad necessitated the need for three ARs per sortie, with a typical mission lasting five hours.

The air armada ranged against Saddam Hussein continued to build, as did the planning on how to deploy such an awesome force to maximum effect. General Chuck Horner, commander of Joint Air Forces (CENTAF) selected a white haired North Carolinan to develop the air campaign, one, Brig Gen Buster Glosson.

An F-4 jock in Vietnam, Glosson's background had a profound impact on the management of Senior Trend during the war planning process. His most memorable experience of the F-117 occurred in 1987, while as commander of the 1st Tactical Fighter Wing, he recalls, "I had spent enough time in the F-15 trying to successfully intercept the F-117, that I was a believer!... The initial twenty four hours of the Gulf War was meticulously planned. I directed the planners to ask themselves three questions about every target they considered, what system had the highest probability of destroying it; what system had the highest probability of its pilot coming back alive, and what system had the highest probability of no civilian casualties. As you may expect, 99% of the

time, the answer to these questions was F-117. We did not have enough F-117s to attack every target. So, I directed the F-117 to be used against the most critical, the most highly defended and difficult-to-hit targets. That gave us the greatest probability of accomplishing our strategic objectives and creating the utmost confusion and disruption. I used all the other systems, be they cruise missiles, fighters or bombers, as fillers."

On 4 December, twenty F-117s from the 416th, 'Ghost Riders', deployed safely to King Khalid, and on the night of the 16/17 January 1991, offensive air operations against Iraq began.

Col Greg Feest recalls the night that validated stealth technology: "The entire first wave of F-117As launched without radio communications, we didn't want the Iraqis to get a 'heads-up' as to our plan. My callsign was Thunder 36 and my wingman, Captain Dave 'Dogman' Francis was Thunder 37. We took off and flew to the tanker without saying a word to each other. My radio was on but remained silent. Since the F-117A is a single-seat fighter, there was no copilot to talk to and the next several hours would be extremely quiet. Having rendezvoused with the KC-135 tankers, we air refuelled and headed North, towards Iraq, while flying on each wing of the tanker. The night was extremely dark and I was thankful, since I did not want the moon to silhouette my jet as I flew into Iraq.

'At approximately 2:30 am, I topped off with fuel, 'stealthed-up' my aircraft and departed the tanker. In 20

Above General Buster Glosson was architect of the Gulf War air campaign. (Buster Glosson)

Right Facilities awaiting the F-117s at King Khalid were second to none. (USAF)

Below This aircraft, in one of the 'canyons' at King Khalid, has a segmented ladder unique to the F-117 operation placed on the aircraft for cockpit access. (USAF)

Below right Aircraft '818, pictured in its Hardened Aircraft Shelter (HAS) at King Khalid completed 38 operational missions during Desert Storm. (USAF)

Below Hal Farley participates in a fly-by in aircraft 831 on 6 December 1990 in preparation for Ben Rich's retirement. (Paul Crickmore)

minutes I would drop the first bomb of Operation Desert Storm. Crossing the Iraqi border, I was nervous as I armed my weapons. My target was an IOC [Intercept Operations Centre] located in an underground bunker, southwest of Baghdad, near Nukhayb. This IOC was a key link between border radar sites and the air defense headquarters in Baghdad. Destroying it would allow other non-stealthy aircraft to enter Iraq undetected.

'Approaching the target I was apprehensive. Two thoughts crossed my mind. First, would I be able to identify the target? Second, did the Air Force really want me to drop this bomb? These thoughts only lasted several seconds.

'I had practised for three years and I could find and destroy any target within one second of my scheduled time-over-target (TOT). Having trained for so long, nothing was going to stop me from dropping my bombs. All I had to do was play, what I called, a highly sophisticated video game, and in 30 minutes I would be back in Saudi Arabia.

'As I approached the target area, my adrenaline was up and instincts took over. My bomb was armed and my systems checked good. I found the target on my infrared (IR) display and concentrated on tracking the target by slewing the cross hairs over the aimpoint. The target had been easier to find than I envisioned. I was able to take time to glance outside the cockpit. Everything was dark except for a few lights in the town. It appeared that no one knew I was in the sky. Looking back at my display, my laser began to fire as I tracked the target. I waited for the display to tell me I was 'in range' and I depressed the 'pickle' button. Several seconds later the weapons bay door snapped open and I felt the 2,000 pound bomb depart the aircraft. The bay door slammed closed as I watched the IR display while continuing to keep the cross hairs on the target. The bomb appeared at the bottom of the display just before it hit. At exactly 2:51 am, I saw the bomb go through the cross hairs and penetrate the bunker. The explosion came out of the hole the bomb had made and blew out the doors of the bunker. I knew I

This page, all GBU-27s were particularly effective against Iraqi HASs. (USAF)

had knocked out the target. The video game was over.

'Having destroyed the target, I turned my aircraft 210 degrees left to head for my second target. While in the turn, I decided to try and see my wingman's bomb hit, since his was due one minute after mine. As I looked back I saw something completely unfamiliar. It looked like fireworks, big bursts of red and orange, flying at me and lighting up the sky. After being stunned for several seconds, I realised it was tracers from triple A. During all my peacetime training missions flying exercises like Red Flag, I had never anticipated what actual triple A would look like. After all it cannot be simulated. I snapped my head forward and pushed the throttles up as far as they would go. I wanted out of the target area as fast as I could.

'As I headed towards my second target, an Iraqi SOC [Sector Operations Centre] at the H-3 airfield in western Iraq, I looked out in front of my aircraft. I now saw what everybody at home saw on television. Tracers, flashes, and flak were all over the place. The whole country had come alive with more triple A than I could ever imagine. I watched several SAMs launch into the sky and fly through my altitude both in front and behind me. But none of them appeared to be guided. Stealth technology really seemed to work! Even if the AAA and SAMs were not guided, the intense 'barrage fire' in my target area was scary. All it would take was a lucky hit.

'I decided to ignore what was happening outside my jet. I lowered my seat and concentrated on my displays. After all, what I couldn't see couldn't hurt me! I dropped my second bomb and turned as fast as I could back towards Saudi Arabia. I don't think I ever manoeuvred the F-117A as aggressively as I did coming off my second target. For a second time in less than 30 minutes, I wanted out of the target area as fast as possible.

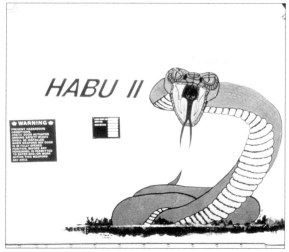

'Having made it safely out of the area, my thoughts turned to my wingman. Dogman was again one minute behind me. I knew he had to fly through the same air defences I had just flown through. I didn't think he would make it. For both of us to survive untouched would require too much good luck."

Having hit both targets, Greg remembers the flight back to King Khalid, "Just prior to crossing the border into Saudi Arabia, I performed my destealth procedures. My task now was to find the post-mission tanker, so I could top off with fuel and make it back to home base. After confirming the tanker was on-station and waiting

Above left and right Nose art was applied inside the F-117's bomb bay doors. 'The Toxic Avenger', Aircraft '813, was the personal mount of Col Al Whitley, Commander of the 37th, during Desert Shield and Desert Storm; the aircraft successfully completed 35 combat missions. Habu II kept the spirit of the SR-71 alive; applied to Aircraft '837, it completed 31 combat missions. (Jim Goodall collection)

Below Aircraft '816 (foreground) was christened 'Lone Wolf' and completed 39 combat missions. (USAF)

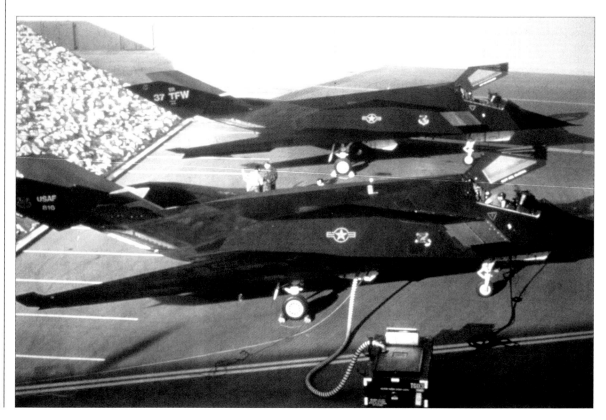

for my 2-ship, I headed for the rejoin point. At a predesignated time, I called Dogman on the radio to see if he was ready to rejoin. I prayed I would hear a response. I didn't hear an answer, so I waited several seconds and tried again. This time I heard him answer. He said he had my aircraft in sight and was ready to rejoin. Now the question was, how many other Stealth Fighters would make it home?"

Today of course we know that all F-117s made it home, not just that night, but every night of the 43-day campaign. On 24 February at 03:00 hours (local), the coalition ground assault began. In true blitzkrieg fashion, it was all over in just three days. On 27 February, Kuwait City was liberated and a ceasefire declared.

After the Storm

Back at Tonopah, arrangements were finalised to relocate the 37th Wing to Holloman AFB, New Mexico (NM). The first aircraft to be delivered was '791, which arrived from Tonopah on 7 January 1992, for maintenance familiarisation. The move officially got underway however on 8 May, when aircraft '814, flown by Lt Col 'Moose' Merritt of the 416th TFS touched down. On 8 July 1992, the 37th FW at Tonopah Test Range took part in an stand down ceremony, and at the same time the 37FW was deactivated and its assets transferred across to the 49FW. Similarly, command of the F-117A wing was also transferred from Col Al Whitley to Brig Gen Lloyd 'Fig' Newton. Unusually however, the squadron designations of the F-117A units remained initially unchanged. The move at last reunited families, enabling them to join their loved ones in living quarters on or close to the base. It also eradicated the need for Key Airlines to shuttle over 2,500 personnel on 75 weekly flights to and from their place of work - a change that would, in itself save millions of dollars a year.

On Tuesday 4 August 1992, the first Holloman based F-117A was lost in an accident. Capt John B Mills of the 416th FS, was forced to eject from Aircraft '801 (not '810 or '802 as reported elsewhere), after it entered an uncommanded roll and caught fire. The crash occurred just eight miles northwest of Holloman; a crash investigation identified the cause as an improperly reinstalled bleed air duct, which led to a hydraulic line malfunction to flight controls and a fire.

Above Col Greg 'Beast' Feest was the first pilot to ever drop a weapon in anger from an F-117. This occurred during Operation Just Cause over Panama. In addition he also released the first bomb to mark the beginning of Operation Desert Storm; by a strange twist of fate, he happened to be flying the same aircraft on both occasions, F-117A, '816. (Col Greg Feest)

Below left Gen Norman Schwarzkopf receives a briefing from Lt Col Ralph Getchell on some of the F-117's intricacies. (USAF)

Below Having been retired from flight test on 11 April 1985, Aircraft '780, the F-117A prototype, became a gate-guard during a ceremony at Nellis AFB on 16 May 1992. (USAF)

The move to Holloman also signalled a steady integration of the F-117A into theatre operational planning, enabling it to become a true 'force multiplier', something impossible to achieve during its years in the black. Accordingly, the 416th participated in Exercise Team Spirit, a short deployment to South Korea. And in June 1993, eight F-117As from the 415th deployed briefly to Gilze-Rijen, in the Netherlands, for Exercise Central Enterprise.

The 49th lost its second F-117A from Holloman, (the fifth to date) on 10 May 1995, at 22:25 hours. Aircraft '822 was being flown by Capt Ken Levens of the 9th Fighter Squadron on a night training flight when contact was lost. The aircraft crashed on Red Mesa, at the Zuri Indian Reservation; the pilot hadn't attempted to eject prior to the crash, and '822 gouged out a 20-foot deep crater upon impact. Having received his bandit number (Bandit 461), on 16 December 1994, Capt Levens had accumulated just 70 hours on the aircraft prior to the incident. An accident investigation team established that there were no signs of mechanical or electrical failure prior to impact and that pilot disorientation seemed, yet again, to be the most likely cause of the tragedy.

The sixth accidental loss of an F-117A occurred publicly and in spectacular fashion. On 14 September 1997, Maj Bryan Knight, an instructor with the 7th FS, flying Aircraft '793, was coming to the end of his expertly choreographed display routine during an airshow at Chesapeake Bay, near Baltimore, Md.. Flying at 380kts and at a height of between 600 and 700 ft, he entered a 15 degree climb when the left outboard elevon made at least four rapid oscillations, causing a 2.5ft section of the inboard elevon to become detached. The aircraft then rolled rapidly left (90 degrees within 0.8 seconds) and pitched sharply up into a high angle of attack. Bryan ejected safely and during the subsequent accident investigation it was determined that the incident had occurred because four Hi-Lok fasteners used to secure the elevon hydraulic actuator to a spanwise, 'Brooklyn Bridge' I-beam, had not been re-installed, following maintenance conducted at Holloman in January 1996.

Flight Test

25 March 1991 saw the completion of a move for F-117 flight test operations from Area 51 to Palmdale. Activity from the new base continued at a brisk pace with Aircraft '831, flown by Lt Col Chris Seat, completing Det.5's first flight from Palmdale the day before. However, the first Senior Trend test sortie from Palmdale was a weapons evaluations flight, flown in Aircraft '784 by Jim Thomas on 23 April 1992.

On the 23 October 1991, a low observability communications study was authorised to identify methods of maintaining communications with an F-117 once it had 'stealthed-up' and retracted all its antennas. The study was completed in February 1992, and on 31 August that same year, Jim Thomas flew Aircraft '783 on its first low observability antenna evaluation sortie. The test program lasted for two months, during which time the 'stealthy antenna', located on the aircraft's underside, was thoroughly evaluated. Following submission of a final report on 13 November 1992, the go-ahead for full scale development of the system was received on 12 May 1993; work commenced four months later, on 16 September, to upgrade the fleet.

Above left On 8 July 1992, Tonopah was deactivated and the 37th moved its F-117s to Holloman AFB, New Mexico. (USAF)

Above With the move from Tonopah to Holloman, came a redesignation and the 37th FW became the 49th FW. Aircraft '816 of the 7th FS is seen overflying the F-117 barns at Holloman. (USAF)

Below Members of the 9th FS, together with their 18 F-117s, form-up behind their boss at that time, Lt Col Greg Feest. (Col Greg Feest)

On 10 October 1994, The Ring Laser Gyro Navigation Improvement Program (RNIP), commenced. Initially designed to evaluate the proposed replacement of SPN-GEANS by the Honeywell H-423 Ring Laser Gyro, the program was subsequently broadened (based on earlier successes achieved by the low observability communication antenna program), to include the addition of a Global Positioning System (GPS). A 'dry bay' was created, by forming a recess in the fuselage fuel tank, on the upper surface of Aircraft '784. Into this was located a stealthy antenna, capable of receiving the relevant satellite generated data. The first RNIP flight occurred on 12 December 1994, and the enhanced accuracy was immediately apparent. This improvement package was incorporated into the entire F-117 fleet. Other benefits offered by the antenna were also exploited, giving rise, in December 1997, to the IRRCA, or Integrated real-time information into the cockpit/Real-time information out of the cockpit, for Combat Aircraft flight test project. Now there's an acronym to test your friends with! By 30 June 1998, the first phase of the program, 'real-time information into the cockpit' had been successfully demonstrated. Phase two, 'real-time information out of the cockpit' began in 1999.

At the heart of IRRCA is the integration of a real-time symmetric multiprocesser, facilitating 1.2 billion instructions per second. As the F-117A receives threat updates from satellite broadcasts, a moving map displays new threats and the processor automatically evaluates the situation. Should analysis of the threat determine that the aircraft is in jeopardy, the processor re-plans the route and displays the option on a new colour liquid crystal diode multi-function display. Decision criteria used in the

Above Another mission begins as this extraordinary geometric study prepares to taxi from its barn. (USAF)

Right An AT-38B of the 7th FS on business at Palmdale. Note the three F-117s on the tail-band. (Paul Crickmore)

Below right F-117 test pilot Jim 'JB' Brown of the 410th Flight Test Squadron, based at Palmdale, readies '784 for another IRRCA test flight. (Paul Crickmore)

proposed re-route includes threat exposure, flying time and landing fuel. The pilot can then accept or reject the proposed option. In addition to mission information, text and images also update the pilot on key events and weather. Evaluations carried out by the 410 Test Squadron at Palmdale indicate that the F-117A is capable of reacting to mission updates or target changes and pop-up threats while still remaining in a stealth configuration.

In early July 1998, Jim 'JB' Brown, lead IRRCA test pilot, flew a simulated combat mission in the dedicated testbed, aircraft '784. During the course of the sortie, a geostationary satellite transmitted a series of encrypted messages to the aircraft via its low-observable communications antenna. These messages included threat updates, mission updates, text information and alternative target imagery. Mission changes provided information for the real-time symmetric multi-processor to re-plan the mission to an alternative target. This was followed by a text message and photos of the alternative target, which enabled 'JB' to verify the processor's planning results and study target details prior to acquisition and attack.

Other Evaluations

Over the years other parties have evaluated the F-117A's capabilities. The first of these being the United States Navy. Two Navy pilots flew the aircraft on eight occasions, during each flight they were chased by an instructor pilot in a T-38. Details of their flight log show that this was a serious evaluation:

PILOT	DATE	A/C SERIAL	TIME	DURATION
Linn	23.10.84	'783	08:38	1.3 hours
Grubbs	23.10.84	'782	13:36	1.4 hours
Linn	24.10.84	'782	13:18	1.6 hours
Linn	25.10.84	'783	08:20	1.6 hours
Grubbs	25.10.84	'783	13:05	1.3 hours
Linn	25.10.84	'782	13:18	1.3 hours
Grubbs	29.10.84	'782	12:33	1.5 hours
Grubbs	31.10.84	'782	13:15	1.4 hours
			Total	11.4 hours

In conclusion of the trials, Lt Cmdr Kenny Linn recalls: "We conducted a thorough performance review, and evaluated the F-117A for suitability in the carrier environment. Unremarkably, it was not suitable at that time for CV use, although it had quite nice handling characteristics in the pattern, landing speeds were too high, and the sink rate limitations were too low. The F-117A had not been built as a CV aircraft, and was not going to turn into one overnight!"

Following the collapse of European Communism, few countries were better placed to successfully complete the transition into a free market economy and democracy than Yugoslavia. However, nationalism, spurred on by the Milosevic regime have conspired to drag the region into 'a new dark age'. The planning and implementation by Serbia of 'Operation Horeshoe' - the systematic 'ethnic cleansing - deportation and genocide - of the Kosovar Albanians, haas once again taken ships and aircraft of NATO to war. At approximately 20:38 (local) on Saturday, 27 March 1999, F-117A, '806, of the 8th FS, flown by Major Dale Zelco, crashed forty miles from Belgrade whilst participating in Operation Allied Force. Although speculation surrounding the loss of this aircraft is rife, nothing has been officially released at the time of writing, other than the fact that Zelco was safely extracted from the area by a combat rescue team.

Above Years of stealth technology were designed into the low visibility of the Lockheed F-22 Raptor. Without black world, no F-22, or at least, many more years of R&D. (Lockheed Martin)

Below Stealth technology is not something reserved solely for military aircraft: witness the Skunk Work's Sea Shadow. (Lockheed Martin)

Epilogue

Since the Skunk Works was founded in 1943, the world has witnessed extraordinary geopolitical changes. Does it therefore follow that the need for 'Skunk Works' type operations in today's world is less now than it was nearly sixty years ago? The author would argue that the need is greater. Such an assertion is made not through some romantic attachment to the aviation pioneers of a bygone era – there is no room for sentiment in today's business world – but rather, it is founded upon the Skunk Works' ability to embrace an ethic of continual change, whether it be in the pursuit of new technologies or the application of operating structures, as set out by Kelly Johnson all those years ago (see below). In August 1992 the Lockheed Advanced Development Company released a summary document entitled 'The Skunk Works' Approach to Aircraft Development, Production and Support,' some of which follows:-

'Over the past few years, we have witnessed sweeping geopolitical changes and revolutionary events that are triggering major changes in our nation's defence requirements. Clearly, in future years, the Defence Department and services will be operating with much smaller force structures and budgets. The resulting challenge will be to maintain a viable, responsive defence infrastructure in the face of budget reductions. To meet this challenge, both the Defence Secretary and Congress are proposing new approaches to DoD acquisition that emphasize research and advanced technologies: technology demonstrators and prototypes; selective upgrading of existing systems; and selective/low rate procurement of new systems.

But not only will we have to develop new technology and systems, we must implement acquisition strategies and management approaches that will enable development and fielding of new systems in a more timely and less costly manner. For the past half century, the Lockheed Skunk Works and its government customers have employed specialized management methods that have done just that…The Lockheed Skunk Works has demonstrated a unique ability to rapidly prototype, develop and produce a wide range of highly advanced aircraft for the US armed forces and intelligence agencies. The P-80, U-2, F-104, SR-71 and, more recently, the F-117 are widely recognised as among the most significant achievements of the aerospace industry.

These and other Skunk Works aircraft have incorporated breakthrough technology to achieve new thresholds in aircraft and systems performance. The common thread among these aircraft is that they were created by men and women working together employing a unique approach to aircraft development – the Skunk Works approach. This management approach, developed by the founder of the Skunk Works C. L. "Kelly" Johnson, fosters creativity and innovation, and has enabled prototyping and development of highly complex aircraft in relatively short time spans and at relatively low cost. It has also demonstrated efficient, economical production of complex systems in small quantities and at low production rates.'

This is of course the skunk standing up for itself, but it is hard to argue with the logic, or the history.

Based on lessons learned from early Skunk Works programs, Kelly Johnson developed and wrote the Basic Operating Rules of the Skunk Works. These fourteen "rules" addressed program management, organization, contractor/customer relationships, documentation, customer reporting, specifications, engineering drawings, funding, cost control, subcontractor inspection, testing, security, and management compensation. Consider rules One to Four:

(1) The Skunk Works' manager must be delegated practically complete control of his program in all aspects. He should report to a division president or higher [In other words, it is essential that the program manager have authority to make decisions quickly regarding technical, finance, schedule, or operation matters.]

(2) Strong but small project offices must be provided both by the customer and contractor [The customer program manager must have similar authority to that of the contractor.]

(3) The number of people having any connection with the project must be restricted in an almost vicious manner. Use of a small number of good people (10 to 25 per cent compared to the so-called normal systems). [Bureaucracy makes unnecessary work and must be controlled brutally.]

(4) A very simple drawing and drawing release system with great flexibility for making changes must be provided. [This permits early work by manufacturing organizations, and schedule recovery if technical risks involve failures.]

All of these rules still make sense. That the Skunk Works has been staffed by the most innovative and talented people in the aerospace industry is beyond dispute – Kelly once remarked to Bob Gilliland, (then Chief Test Pilot of the SR-71) "I'm a prima donna and I'm surrounded by prima donnas."

Latterly, Lockheed has performed well, buying up in the process Martin Marietta and General Dynamics. With a management hierarchy in all three companies, there is a clear need to consolidate. The new president of this empire is Dain Hancock, from the General Dynamics Corporation's F-16 Fighting Falcon program. When Jack Gordon, president of the Skunk Works suddenly announced that he was retiring, he was replaced by another ex-GD man, Robert T Elrod, who holds a master's degree in business administration. Paul Martin, former Skunk Works executive vice president, has also gone. Gary Grigg, a company spokesman confirmed that: "There may not be as many skunk logos on the buildings when we repaint them".

When a new Chief Executive is appointed to any large corporation, they invariably come with their own agenda and 'baggage', gathered from past experiences. In the author's opinion, it would be a disaster of terrible proportions, maybe for the company, maybe for the US, maybe for the world, if president Hancock's agenda included dismantling the Skunk Works by stealth.